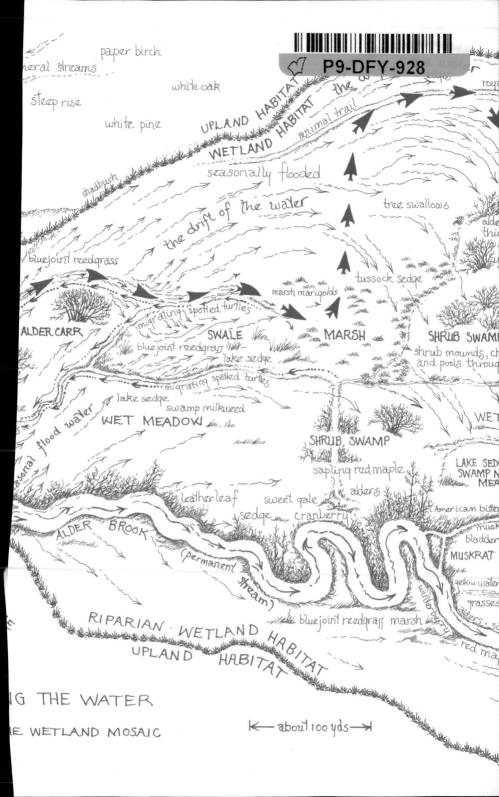

paper birch

eral streams

white oak

Steep rise

white pine

UPLAND HABITAT the

WETLAND HABITAT animal trail

seasonally flooded

shadbush

the drift of the water

tree swallows

alde
this

bluejoint reedgrass

tussock sedge

marsh marigolds

ALDER CARR

migrating spotted turtles

SWALE

MARSH

SHRUB SWAMP

bluejoint reedgrass

shrub mounds, ch
and pools throug

lake sedge

migrating spotted turtles

lake sedge

swamp milkweed

WET MEADOW

WET

SHRUB SWAMP

LAKE SED
SWAMP N
MEA

sapling red maple

leatherleaf

sweet gale

alders

American bitter

sedge

cranberry

mus
bladder

ALDER BROOK

MUSKRAT

(permanent

yellow water

stream)

grasses

alders s

bluejoint reedgrass marsh

red ma

RIPARIAN · WETLAND HABITAT

UPLAND HABITAT

G THE WATER

E WETLAND MOSAIC

← about 100 yds →

BOOKS BY DAVID M. CARROLL

The Year of the Turtle
Trout Reflections
Swampwalker's Journal
Self-Portrait with Turtles
Following the Water

FOLLOWING THE WATER

A Hydromancer's Notebook

∽⦿⦿∾

DAVID M. CARROLL

*per carissima Maria Angela —
dearest friend of so many
years (molti, ma molti
anni) — constant supporter
& encourager, with thanks
and love.
baci, abbracci, amore
David*

*David M. Carroll
August 2009*

Houghton Mifflin Harcourt
Boston New York
2009

For information about permission to reproduce selections from this book,
write to Permissions, Houghton Mifflin Harcourt Publishing Company,
215 Park Avenue South, New York, New York 10003.

www.hmhbooks.com

Library of Congress Cataloging-in-Publication Data
Carroll, David M.
Following the water : a hydromancer's notebook / David M. Carroll.
p. cm.
ISBN 978-0-547-06964-7
1. Wetland ecology—New Hampshire. 2. Wetlands—
New Hampshire. 3. Natural history—New Hampshire.
4. Carroll, David M.—Homes and haunts. I. Title.
QH105.N4C267 2009
577.6809742'72—dc22
2008052951

Book design by Lisa Diercks
Typeset in Monotype Fournier

Printed in the United States of America
DOC 10 9 8 7 6 5 4 3 2 1

Several chapters of this book appeared, in somewhat different form, in *Tufts
Magazine* (Winter 2007) under the title "Scenes from the End of a Season."

Lines from "Villa at the Foot of Mount Chungnan" by Wang Wei, from
Anthology of Chinese Poetry, edited by Wai-Lim Yip. Copyright © 1997 by Duke
University Press. Used by permission of the publisher. All rights reserved. Lines
from "Escondido en los muros" by Luis Cernuda, from *The Poetry of Luis
Cernuda: Order in a World of Chaos,* by Neil Charles McKinlay (London: Tamesis,
1999). Used by permission of the publisher. All rights reserved.

For Meredith, Harry, and Jim

FOLLOWING THE WATER

YEARBREAK

AT THE EARLIEST openings of the ice in the overwintering niches of the spotted turtles, as minute glimmers of quickening water appear in acres of wetlands still locked in ice and snow, I forsake my winter paths: the worn floor by the kitchen table and fireplace; the even more worn threshold of the narrow doorway to the Oriental-carpeted passage down the back hall, the narrow gallery hung with paintings and drawings above agreeably overburdened bookcases, lined along the floor with stacks of more books and empty frames; the footworn stair treads up to my studio workrooms, with their slender passageways among bookcases, drawing and writing tables, and shelves, all impossibly piled with papers, notebooks, pencils, pens, and paintbrushes. With the opening up of the earth and water I go beyond my few, close-to-home outer trails of the cold season: my way to the woodshed, as trodden as an ancient deer path, and my modest snowshoe circlings through the back field and bordering woods. At thaw I begin to walk a wider way again, beyond house and gardens, in places every bit as home to me as those.

Some of my paths are of my own making, many are borrowed from deer and muskrat; most are routes that water traces. In some of these water-and-mud channels my feet drop into hollows exactly matching my strides: my own footprints of previous years' passings. In rare places left alone enough, generations of black bears walk historic migration routes in the impressed footprints of their ancestors.

Stepping from a snow-crested bank, I descend into the icy running of the brook. There is the daybreak that comes with every rising of the sun, and there is the yearbreak that comes with thaw and the unlocking of the ice. As I enter the newly opened water, I enter the year and, in a mingling of dream clearly remembered and new dream just beginning, start to wade again the streaming of its seasons.

The turbulent whitewater spates of mid-March have run their course. Floods may be brought surging back to life by April rains and the last of the snowmelt from headwater hills, escaping the banks again and surging through the low white pine terrace, the alder and meadowsweet thickets, the red maple swamp. But for now the brook has settled back within its channel and is not so restless that I cannot see into it. Insulated by neoprene, I wade in. For the first time in the year I move within the variously black, sky-reflecting, and (where shadows allow my sight to penetrate its masking surface) clear, clear flowing of the stream.

At another winter's ending I have one more setting forth, one more initiation. Though I am always one year older, the year is ever new, renascent. I leave the past cold season, a time passed largely in the theater of my own mind, my inner wilderness, leaving it behind like a skin I have sloughed, and enter the wild realm that lies outside of myself and ultimately outside of all human knowing. But my new skin bears the same markings as before, and whatever I encounter within the season extending before me will be at once familiar and completely new.

As I have somehow known from my first intuitive setting out, I will recognize what to follow. The water will set a course and lead me through the days; the days will take me through the year. I go forth directed and open to direction. What guides the feet? the mind? the heart? The heart, too, is forever seeking.

I once brought a naturalist friend, one whose quests range as widely over the planet as mine keep to a circumscribed corner within it, to some of the places that have been at the heart of what I have followed in the wild over the past three decades. I introduced her to a vernal pool, a marsh, a swamp, a stream, and along the way I found some turtles to show her. I talked some, of what I see, what I look for.

"They say that the Sufi is always looking for his beloved," she said. "You are always seeking your beloved."

My first heading out of the year always takes me back to the first time I wandered out, the beginning of my being there. I felt that I was called, that something called me, and I set out alone. That was in my eighth year, when spring was turning to summer. In every year following, that feeling has come at ice melt, when I go out to see the stream at its first running clear, see the water in marshes and swamps at the moment of opening up, trembling with the restless stirrings of the air at the time of great transition—water set free, vibrant and vibrating, shimmering back to the sun, the heart-melting light of spring's awakening. The touch of the ascendant sun on ice at length gives birth to water, and water gives life to the year. After winter's silence, countless dialogues begin. I set out to see if the water has come back, always with the hope, mingled with anticipation, of seeing the first turtle. In the renewal of the year I can find again that first turtle, take it in with my eyes, touch it with my fingertips. Could a year begin for me without this? My life has come to be measured in first turtles.

As I wade against the steady, at times insistent, flow, I

think back to my earliest experiences with this liquid mineral, now clear, now silver or amber, gold, black, deep wine red, or tannic tea, so alive and life-sustaining within its fundamentally physical, utterly indifferent nature. Water nurtures beyond the purely physical. As a boy I entered waters that, if not alive themselves, were so filled with light and life that my binding with them was as much metaphysical as physical. These primal immersions took place in small still-water marshes and swamps and running brooks too minimal to serve the prodigiously expanding economic and recreational needs and desires of mankind. These places of my boyhood continued to hold something of the heart of wildness in a landscape being stripped of all original meaning. Not yet subject to human usurpation and engineering, they were the soul of the seasons, the lifeblood of ecologies. They were wild out of all proportion to their scale in the landscape, and they imparted wildness to my boyhood heart and mind, my youthful imagination.

But over time so many of these watery places, even the least of them, were driven into corners, becoming heavily compromised relicts marginalized out of their existential meaning, if not out of existence. These were my baptismal waters. For all that they gave me—the beauty and the belonging, the intuitive knowledge of something of my place in life, becoming something that I simply could not live without—I think sometimes of the heartache, the anger and despair, that I would have been spared, had that entrance into the water not opened, had I not entered. Their loss is overwhelming. With every passing year, my following of the water has increasingly become a matter of finding water to follow.

Streamside thickets and occasional taller trees along the stream write their signatures on the water, an undulating script on an ever-moving page. Even these shadows have their identities: the whiplike lines of silky dogwood, broader trailings of alder stems, bolder strokes of red maple trunks, and sweeps of white pine crowns. Are these shadows or transparent reflections? They cut narrow slits and wider openings in the clear water, which the light of day would mask. I shift my head, looking in from as many different angles as possible, trying to catch sight of a wood turtle, tucked in or perhaps even shifting about, as sometimes happens as the long overwintering approaches its conclusion, even when the brook is only four degrees above freezing. But it is enough to see the streambed again, its sand, cobble, and stones, sunken branches and drifts of leaves.

I raise my head and look upstream. Can I be looking at a wood turtle? The shape is far enough ahead that I cannot be certain, and my disbelief that a turtle would be so exposed, up on an open, muddy mound of stream bank surrounded by snow and ice, prevents definite recognition. But as I advance I begin to read it as a turtle, and the reading is disturbing. The angle, something in the way that so-familiar sculpted shape is settled, is sharply out of keeping with any search-image I have. Wood turtles always place themselves in harmony with their surroundings, with the configurations of the earth or stream bottom on which they have settled or over which they move. This gestalt has struck me as unfailing. Except when they are compelled to cross a road or open lawn, wood turtles are never out of place.

Even from some distance, as I wade, looking into the turtle's face, I know that something is terribly wrong. Where is that light in the eyes, the light of life and reflected day that shows before the gold-ringed eyes themselves can be clearly seen? What are those shadows, dark pockets on either side of the jet black head? Where are the legs, black-scaled, with vivid flashes of red-orange skin color that should be part of the pattern? Riveted by this troubling vision, I never look away as my feet find their way over the streambed and I wade to the turtle. A profound confusion comes over me, the elation of seeing that first turtle up out of the water at the end of hibernation mingling with a reality I do not want to see. The turtle's eyes are closed, her legs are gone.

I pick her up. Her shell is so familiar, that shadowy umber brown carapace with yellow-gold striations, like faint flecks of sunlight. Tiny notches I have made along her marginal scutes identify her. An adult female, she is one of the first wood turtles I documented along this brook, where I have been recording them in notebooks over the past twenty years. Her head does not move, there is no sign of life in her tail as I move it from side to side. A few tiny bubbles appear at her nostrils, perhaps a last flicker of life. All of her right front leg is missing and the lower half of her left front. Her right hind leg has been eaten away from the knee joint down, and her left hind leg is only a shaft of bone to where the knee joint was. How did she get up here? My crowded thoughts and questions settle out, and I realize that of course she could not have climbed up onto this mound but was left here by the otter who discovered her in her winter hold in the stream and wrestled her onto land to work at her, force out at least a foot to eat from the fortress of her shell. There is not one tooth mark on her carapace or plastron; predators know there is no biting through the shell of a wood turtle this size.

A sense of foreboding comes over me, as it did five years ago when, at this same seasonal moment, I discovered an adult male who had lost both front legs and then a six-year-old who had been bitten through and killed. I am familiar with reports by others who study turtles of heavy losses on colonies of painted and snapping turtles by otters preying upon them during their hibernation. I found no further evidence of such predation that year, but I wonder what I will find when the wood turtles here begin their first streamside basking of this new season.

I set the turtle back down. The temperature will drop well below freezing tonight. If the least flicker of life does remain within her, it will be extinguished. A life of decades, likely more than half a century, has come to an end. Borrowed stardust is at length returned, and the flame that burned within passed on. In silence, the water flows on by.

Otter and hidden wood turtle.

Alder shadows creep across the snow. This is an aspect of what takes place in the stream, along its banks and beyond. My human-turtle connection does not allow me complete objectivity. But my deepest griefs are human-driven, not by the death of any individual living thing within the ecology, but that of the ecology itself.

WRITING APRIL

1 APRIL. The crowns of the royal fern mounds have melted free, but they are islands of pale ocher and sienna (warm in color and in what they collect from the sun), outposts of thaw in the encircling acres of ice and mounds of snow that still prevail throughout the great alder carr.

Winds, strong and chill, stir that familiar, near-at-hand rustling in the dry sedges, as though something with more substance than wind were moving through them. Distant low roar in the upland pines beyond the swamp. Not long ago I heard a few red-winged blackbird calls, distant and windblown, coming from the border of the brook.

· · ·

Woodcocks know the snow's first melting away from the bases of alder mounds, the slightest openings achieved by upwelling groundwater and seeps in the alder carr and aspen thickets; all of life is intimately attuned to the narrowest of margins.

Deer tracks are set in the footprints I left in the lingering snowpack at the edge of the swamp yesterday. I so often take to deer trails; here one has taken to mine, step for step.

Wading among the sallows, a broad swath of just-over-head-high willow shoots at the outer edge of the deeply flooded alder swamp, I see a pair of black ducks leave silver streaks on the dark water as they stealthily, silently glide out of sight. Secure in the same screening blur of emergent shrubs, the ducks, of a species that is ever alert and seems to be always on edge, do not burst into the air in wild-winged flight, their almost invariable reaction upon catching sight of me. Losing myself among the countless fine branches, I enter one of those watery thickets in which everything but the present moment and place is brushed away from me. I can feel myself disappearing. My awareness shifts to the pliant stems immediately surrounding me.

As my focus turns to the just-emerging catkins, their bud scales and leaf buds still pressed tight against lustrous stems, I become seeing eyes and touching hands only. A

Sallows.

song sparrow sings and I become listening ears as well. In the maze of wandlike branches above the floodwater, runoff, and melted snow that have escaped the banks of the brook to inundate this hollow, I read the supple growth of the willows, stem by stem. As they assume the colors of quickening life, they vary within their own species and among the three or so species that grow here. Some stems are green-gold, streaked with a sheen of sunlight. Others are gray-green, a rich umbered purple, or dull ocher-green mottled with a smoky charcoal gray. The tiny leaf scales range from greens to carmine.

The scales of the flower buds respond to the season. Some have almost imperceptibly separated from their branches to show tips of fine white silk. Others have opened almost fully to unveil soft catkins—pewter gray, silver, ivory white. The scales that have sheltered these flower buds through the winter fall away as I brush among their stems. Willow catkins—first flowers of thaw in the shrub swamps and along the borders of brooks, belonging to the wind and water of winter's fitful transition to spring, nascent in a new-born season, open to wild pollinators.

I begin to wade out of the alder carr. My left foot has gone numb. The wind has abated, and red-winged blackbirds have advanced into the alder thickets. Their evensongs ring clearly in my ears. A mourning dove's plaintive calls descend from a high pine on the upland ridge. I hear Canada geese trumpeting but cannot make them out against the low sunlit sky to the west. As I scan for them, I hear that familiar rain of twittering, then see a flock of tree swallows wheeling directly overhead. A great blue heron departed from the marsh beyond the alder lowlands as I entered them, and on my way here I heard a phoebe and a robin. In leaving the shrub carr I cut a wand of beaked hazelnut on which the tassels have lengthened in the time since I walked in. The threadlike, bright magenta tips of the female flowers are showing, familiar signs that the season has come back in a day.

It will be a while before I see the next spotted turtle or the first vernal-pool amphibians. Cold, blustery winds and a dusting of snow in the night. North by northwest winds are blowing a smoke of snow from the high white pines. A cardinal sings, but it is cold, a winter's-edge day in early April sun, the sky a hard, cold blue.

Water-murmur and the distant evening song of a robin. The high crowns of the pussy willow thicket have come into full bloom. The sun has slipped behind the western hills as unrelenting winds bring a snow squall down from the mountain. The snow melts upon touching the stream bank, dissolves as it swirls into the brook.

· · ·

The run of chill, wind-blasted days and nights of hard frost continues. There is no sun. Sharp-toothed winds whistle along the little silver-running brook that divides the gray-trunked, low, level expanse of the red maple swamp, gray trunks accentuated by the muted yet radiant gray-green glowing of lichens in a time of cool, abundant moisture. The maples rock and clatter together on high, where a few first flowers open. Several trees reach up from each stump left after the last cutting in the swamp. Ancient roots, perennial enough to seem eternal, could send up new sprouts following cuttings by man or beaver every year for decades until, left alone for a time, they become trees again and reclaim their forest.

As I approach the grassy vernal pool in the late afternoon, I hear a deafening chorus of wood frogs and peep frogs ringing out. Within this ear-impacting din I can make out the rollicking splash of the wood frogs. The power of the midday sun working on water in mid-April: when I passed by here just four and a half hours ago I heard only a few tentative calls. Now those isolated eruptions that seemed to be questions have been answered. I wade among the wood frogs as they leap and roll through the deeper trench just out from the emergent winterberry thicket, their traditional site for depositing two enormous communal egg masses each spring. The frogs do not perform their customary multitude-in-unison disappearing act; they have become too aroused by their own inner fire—perhaps a strange concept, since they are deemed in human terms "cold-blooded"— and by the heat of the season to pay any heed to my approach or my stationary looming over them. But they do take immediate notice as a bittern wings low over their orgy. This consummate frog predator, who can rise up out of nowhere even when there appears to be no standing cover, puts them down in an instant, abruptly silencing their tumult. The peep frogs shrill on. I imagine the bittern has been feeding well on the incautious male wood frogs. They will soon get their wits about them and resume their silent and secretive ways. For now they are the image and sound of wild abandon at the "at-last" breaking of spring.

Late in the day a robin sings incessantly, and a mourning dove calls repeatedly from the dense pine stand above the alder carr. Only the faintest sunlight shows in the alders, as the sun is about to disappear in the hazy sky, dropping beneath the pines of the low western horizon. It is breathless here, but as so often happens, I hear the wind in the high white pines to the east. Now robins call from roundabout, their distant, lilting song to the sun's setting and rising. Piercing even from across this great alder swamp, the calls of the red-winged blackbirds mingle with those of the robins. Sapling red maples here and there among the alders spike the maroon-gray thickets with sharp red, the color of April's coming to life. This, the time of the red maple flowering, is the best time here and throughout the swamps and river floodplains, along the brooks and streams, wherever water stands or flows. After all these years I try to fill up on this signal moment, but there is no keeping it. It always comes to this: I can only return, again and again, and be here in this too-brief time. The temperature drops quickly, sharply, with the setting of the sun.

I don't think I've ever heard a more massive—if this word can be applied to sound—chorusing of wood frogs and spring peepers. It pulses directly into the skull, one has no need of ears. Standing in the full brunt of it, I feel that I risk hearing impairment. What it does to the mind, the heart, is my kind of maddening . . . no, my kind of wildening.

The ringing in my ears fades as I move away, but I walk from chorus to chorus; just as I move out of range of hearing the wood frogs, and as the peep frogs become faint, I pick up the outer fringe of the same heart-gladdening communal crescendo from the vernal pool by the boglike border of the marsh. It is exhilarating to enter into the full sweet fury of this singing and have it fall away as I leave it behind, only to pick up another, ahead in the cranberry–sweet gale meadow that is my destination. To live in a landscape where one could never outwalk the wild callings of spring . . .

A BREATH AT THAW

IN THE WOODS and over the great plain of the hayfield there are still two to four feet of snow—another year in which I have to snowshoe to the first open water other than that which has been set free in brooks and rivers. In the shrub-swamp compartment of the great alder carr, the slow, steady drift of floodwater from the distant stream and the heat-collecting melange of rampant vegetation combine to erode the ice. The first open water and the first turtles—spotted turtles—appear at the same time, often on the same day, in this small, sedge-crowded first foothold of thaw in a vast landscape still lying beneath a mantle of winter white.

My year within the year, the year of the turtle, begins

here. The ice is less than a day off the water. Knowing that I am so near that moment, I step down from ice and snow and wade into the season. I always hold the thought, anticipation-cum-hope, that I will see a turtle in the very act of emerging from hibernation and will recognize it as such. I have come close and perhaps even witnessed it in essence. Certainly I have envisioned it, that astonishing appearance from a half year's darkness, the awakening from that deepest of vertebrate sleeps, the coming forth from mud and intertwined roots and rhizomes of shrubs and sapling red maples anchored on atolls of royal fern mounds into clear, cold water filled with light, and then the critical ascent to open air and the warmth of the sun.

After that near-interminable abiding, it all begins so quickly with the turtles. What are the dreams, if any, between the closing of the eyes in one year and their opening in another? What is this sleep of stillness that can last for half a year, the state of being of all living things, from turtles to alders, that do not migrate or are not active in winter but stay in place and wait? The transformation that at times seems as if it will never happen can take place in surprisingly short order: ice and snow are changed into water, and winter is converted to spring. April completes the work that March began, and the year and the turtles within it are on the move.

Is it possible to truly understand what triggers this, what

precise timing arises from an interaction between life and nonliving elements: turtle, mud and water, temperature, time itself? I have long felt that somehow, even in deepest hibernation, turtles always know where the sun is and where their corner of the spinning Earth is in relation to it. What else is involved? How has life, among its countless ideas, or solutions, come to this yet one more remarkable, and in the end unfathomable, expression of itself?

I stand at that great division of the northern year, grateful that the critical place is still here and that I can come here to meet the moment one more time. For many years I have stood at thaw, in water or on shrub and fern mounds, watching for long unmoving spells, thinking I might see that initial movement, the instant of appearance, waiting . . . giving something a chance to happen before my eyes.

Could this be it? I do not witness the emergence from the substrate beneath the water, but something catches my peripheral vision, and my head turns involuntarily to see a spotted turtle where a moment before there was none. It must be possible to witness that fraction of time I seek, but the instant is set in so much possible time and space, even on the narrowest edge of thaw in a relatively constricted opening in a shrub swamp.

There is a directness in the slow movements of the turtle across the mucky bottom of one of the channels to the base of a mound formed by royal fern and alder and his subsequent ascent of its slope. There is no cautious pause to look around from just beneath the surface before raising his head above the water nor vigilant scanning after doing so before beginning his climb out of it. The turtle proceeds to haul himself halfway out of the water, extends his neck full length, thrusts back his head, and opens his mouth. His throat bellows out—I am amazed at the extent of it.

After the long, deep elemental breath—I have to think it is his first in nearly six months—I expect the turtle to crawl up onto the mound to bask. But after the turtle lowers his head, he pauses for only several seconds before quickly rotating to his left, slipping from the mound, and beginning to swim away. Once again I am surprised by the turtle's alacrity, by what appears to be a virtually immediate recovery, restoration. Can one breath, no matter how deep— and I have to think that that first breath is taken at times when the tips of the nostrils are just above the surface— take away the effects of an unbreathing winter, a time spent essentially insensate, encased within his shell, withdrawn into his own bones with no external needs while his heart marked the time until thaw at some eight beats per minute? For a moment I think of all the living breaths that have been taken in the world.

I capture the turtle, hold him just long enough to identify him for my notes and also simply to touch him—a

naturalist's documentation and my personal experience. Ultimately I cannot justify even the briefest intervention but take him in hand. I cannot fully touch the season until I touch a turtle.

RETURN TO THE
WOOD-TURTLE STREAM

HEAVY RAINS, mixed at times with sleet: a cold, dark mid-April spell and the return of floodwaters have kept me from the brook for more than a week. But April's familiar vacillations between winter and spring are not alone responsible for my absence. I have taken them as an excuse for not returning, as in my uneasiness my mood has matched that of the weather and kept me from taking advantage of the few breaks for walking the stream banks in search of turtles. The mingled elation and dread that move through me at the season's outset are a mix as turbulent as the brook at thaw. Irresistible attraction collides with a deeply deterring apprehension, and in this dynamic I become paralyzed. It can no longer be for me as it was in those first few years in boyhood, in which I could not see what was coming and never stopped to think that swamps and streams might not be forever.

Each spring I see, in addition to landscapes lost entirely, the increasingly tight encirclement of and encroachment upon this and so many other turtle places. Concomitantly, in "protected" places not eradicated outright by development, comes the inevitable entering and overrunning by the human world. I have long witnessed the invasion that takes the heart from the landscape, and it has taken much of the heart from me. Increasingly in my later years of following the water, following the turtles, I have had to turn away. Sometimes I stay away for an extended time, and there are places to which I cannot return at all.

But where wildness lingers and turtles hold within it, that original searching, that early unquestioned need to be there, draws me back. For me, the most compelling occasions over the course of the seasons are the first appearance of the spotted turtles as they emerge from hibernation; the wood turtles' first coming up onto stream banks after that same long sleep; turtle-nesting time; and the nest-emergence and nest-to-water journeys of the hatchling wood turtles. These seasons within the season have beckoned me powerfully enough to overcome my ever-deepening reluctance. But even these holds erode. I never would have believed that I could deny their calling, but more frequently with each passing year I am drawn forth only to be driven back. As I come to this wooded brook today, my agitation is intensified by the unshakable image of the dead, legless turtle on the wintry stream bank in late March: image as portent.

The extent and force of the last flood surge, which reached its height several days ago, is manifest in the record it has left in snags, collections of interwoven branches, leaves, pine needles, strands of sedge, grass, and vine, looking like windrows throughout the lowlands. The debris caught in ironwood and alders tells me that I would have been chest-deep in water then. Some flood wrack has built up so high I cannot step over it but must circle around, as I approach the brook, which has once again settled within its banks and quieted considerably.

I wade in clear water flowing over scoured sand, a stream alive with amber webbings of April sunlight, then on down a swift-running riffle over cobble to climb a bank lined by alders, silky dogwood, and northern arrow-wood, flanked in turn by extensive thickets of meadowsweet. As I crouch and rise, continually shift my point of view, look ahead and then turn to look back the way I came, I see a wood turtle not far upstream who is visible only from a very specific angle. She basks in a classic edge-of-the-stream setting that is emblematic of the season for me, and although I have many photographs of just such a scenario, I take another series as I approach her.

I pick her up. Everything seems perfect, the feel of that sun-warmed shell, the familiar weight and density that is so surprising in a turtle that has gone nearly half a year without eating. Only when I turn her over in my hands do I see that she has lost the lower half of her right front leg. The amputation was surely the work of an otter, probably during her overwintering. A turtle I have documented in past notebooks, she had lived here for twelve years without incident, not so much as a tail nip, until this wound. It will heal. I am well aware that these turtles are remarkably resistant to bleeding to death or getting infections, even from multiple amputations, and that in many cases a wood turtle can sustain this degree of limb loss and go on for many years. But my sense of foreboding only deepens.

I turn upstream and soon find another turtle, this one on a sandbar building up on the inside turn of a deep-bend meander in the brook. An older male, he is settled at the base of a lodging of beaver-trimmed branches I had left last fall as a supply of wading staffs for this season. I am surprised that the flood did not carry them away. Even before picking him up I know that he too has fallen victim to a predatory otter. There is nothing left of his left front leg, and only the merest stub of his right front leg remains. He has shoved himself here with his hind feet. Immediately I think of the imminent mating season: if he lives on—and it is possible that even in this terribly compromised condition he will survive—I do not see how he could successfully do battle with another male during the often fierce combats they stage at breeding time or how he could manage to pursue and mount a female. But he is an adult male wood turtle and will go on trying to do what he has done before, everything he exists to do.

Does he even know that those powerful forelegs are no longer there? Perhaps not, or perhaps he has some awareness that all is not the same. After recording him I set him down. He shuffles back into his basking hollow and doesn't move again. In the past, after being disturbed he would have scrambled into the brook and surged off through the water with strong strokes of all four legs.

A turtle leg—or even two or all four—seems so little sustenance for a predator such as a river otter. And it is such a great loss for an animal as long-lived as a turtle. But that is my reckoning, as one partial to turtles. Ever impartial, nature does not calculate on such a scale in seeking to maintain its temporal equilibriums, which are staged against constant challenge. A turtle leg may help an otter continue along to a deeper feeding; a turtle must evade or overcome the consequences of predation.

Thinking of the adult female who is the most familiar to me of all those I follow or observe here, in that I have seen her more times over more years than any other, I continue upstream. I am well acquainted with her rounds of the year, her seasonal times and places. In my apprehensive approach to a small stretch of the brook that curls around the peninsula of a red maple swamp where she spends her winters, I see her. I find that she has lost her entire right front leg and most of her left hind foot. My documentation becomes excruciating. I realize that these findings are forcing me to become purely a field biologist collecting data; the writing down becomes numbing. She will be ambulatory at least, and perhaps capable of nesting.

Soon after this I find another male who has lost a leg, and then an older male, one of the colony's dominants, perhaps even an alpha male, who on the turning of a moment has been left with but one small stub where his two broad forelegs, so characteristic of fully mature males, had propelled him through decades.

I hesitate before walking on . . . can I go on witnessing, recording this unprecedented predation? I remind myself that what I have encountered is not the result of some human-driven assault. In this essentially natural arena I am witness to a harsher aspect of life pitted against life, in the form of two very different species arrived at by widely divergent evolutionary pathways. Those paths of biological destiny have brought otter and wood turtle to this brook at this moment in the streaming of time and to a clash of fates set in the coevolutionary process. The otter survives through rapacious predation, the turtle by avoiding or surviving it.

Reality presses hard upon the dream of the new season. I try to accommodate both and stay with the day and all that unfolds within it. My turning all but completely to my field ecologist aspect is in no small measure an act of self-preservation, a way to suppress my boyhood turtle-seeking, swamp-and-stream-wandering-in-forgetfulness, which was what brought me to my original connection and dominated my early decades and which has never left me nor been driven out of me.

It becomes clear that I am seeing the results of an unusual predatory episode. I have to think that there were more fatalities than the one I witnessed, and it occurs to me that dead turtles may well have been swept along by the floods and perhaps ended up in the assemblages of debris left throughout the brook-side lowlands. I begin to search, and almost at once I see a shell sticking upright from a lengthy barrier that has the appearance of a fence made of wattles wedged up against a row of alders. Far from what I came here to look for today, this is a necessary finding. I know I have to see this search through and document as completely as possible whatever it reveals.

It does not always happen that something I have envisioned, for good or ill, so quickly comes to pass. But it occurs often enough that it could seem preternatural: my seeing in advance seems destined. This intuition—or is it merely the entertaining of a hunch?—is more likely a case of the predictable arising from accumulated experience than it is pure chance or anything psychic. It has much to do with cues in the seasonal situation and has its foundation in the natural. My observations have led me to be in full accord with the aphorism that the eye seldom sees what the mind does not anticipate. Sometimes, as in the upright turtle shell before me, the anticipated appears with what seems impossible immediacy. At other times years pass between the envisioning and the seeing. In either case what I have foreseen uncannily appears all but exactly as I expected. And I never stop looking.

A little more than half of the shell juts perpendicularly from the compacted matrix of flood debris. I look down into it to see that the forelegs are intact, folded and drawn into the shell to block the narrow space between the carapace and the plastron, in the manner of a wood turtle protecting his head. Limbs can be lost, and life goes on, but a bite to the head—the favored modus operandi of a terrestrial predator, the raccoon—is fatal. Perplexed by the perfect condition of the forelegs, and almost without thinking, I take a twig to touch one. The leg flinches—the turtle is alive.

When I pull her from the debris a story comes together: she has no hind legs. A living turtle, not a lifeless shell, was swept along with and integrated into this snag of branches, vines, leaves, and long strands of grass and sedge, the very stuff of the cover that these turtles are utterly dependent on to pass unseen by predators. In a terrible twist of fate, a large female wood turtle, deprived of the strong legs and gripping feet and claws that would anchor her during the most insistent surges of the brook or allow her to escape from the

full force of a spate and secure a holdfast in a quieter edge or backwater, became no more than a piece of driftwood carried along by the flood. She was left entangled in such a way that her intact forefeet could find no leverage, and she had no hind legs with which to extricate herself.

It is hard to see how she can go on. I set her down, step back, and watch. Her head comes out. She looks about her, regarding the world with which she has an intimacy, a history, and connections I cannot imagine. In time her forelegs extend . . . that beautiful, deep orange color. No hind legs will ever appear again from that sculpted shell. Can she pull herself along, get by somehow? She begins to move, and I am startled by the leverage she achieves. I crouch down to observe, and see that the merest stump of her left hind leg is just barely able to touch the ground and provide her with a modicum of thrust. Her progress is not as agonizing as I had pictured.

I think again of coevolutionary design, of how everything around me here is still being worked on, worked out, as has been the case since life's beginnings on Earth. That opening between the rear edges of the turtle's carapace and plastron has been shaped to allow her to withdraw her legs and tail. Living bone, the rib cage, has been remarkably modified to shield legs and tail from a range of predatory teeth and claws. And the degrees of dexterity and movement of those teeth and claws have in turn evolved to overcome a vast suite of deterrents and defenses, among them the legendarily protective shell of the turtle. Teeth and claws cannot overcome all defenses all the time, turtle shell is not always invulnerable. This endless play of one capacity or strategy against another goes on and will continue as long as life persists.

But here I see that the narrow opening guarding legs and tail allows, in the case of a failure of that defense, the least stump of a leg to extend to the ground and provide a degree of locomotion. If arrived at by chance, such an adaptation is, by means of an endless succession of survival tests, ever being engineered in the direction of perfection of form and function. A complexity beyond comprehension is involved in this one matter alone, but I believe I am looking at evidence of the turtle shell shaping predatory mouth and paw, and predatory mouth and paw influencing the design of the shell.

The turtle is clearly challenged. If she lives on she will mate, but she will never be able to nest again. And if she falls on her back she may not be able to right herself, and so will die the same long, slow death that would have been her fate had I not found her trapped in the flood debris. I see in her situation another face of evolutionary reality: how a remarkable survivability, a complex complement of adaptations that is essential to the species' persistence, can put an individual of that species to the most severe tests. I cannot think of another vertebrate animal that could have survived the days she spent trapped in flood debris. The turtle's capacity for going without food, even water—occasional rain probably kept her going in her all-but-certainly fatal predicament—for protracted periods might well have allowed her to linger for weeks.

If another predator had found her and tried to extract her head or a leg, it might have pulled her from the snag and then, failing to get anything out of her shell, wandered off, freeing her in turn to hobble on. Such interactions of chance and design, played out over a span of time I cannot grasp, must play a role in the history of life on Earth. It is a history that, as Thoreau observed, we erase without ever having come close to fully reading.

The days, possibly years, left to her will be framed in struggle. But she can go on, and for whatever time she has left, I resolve to allow her to live it here rather than in some protective captivity. If she can gain this much leverage on the smooth surface of the flood-plastered leaves where I set her, she will be able to move about her territory. As compromised as she is, I am certain she will be able to find plants to eat and slugs, the favorite food of wood turtles.

It is nearly impossible for me to do so, but I turn back to the stream, where I quickly come upon another turtle, yet one more amputee. An old male has only one small stub to serve as forelegs. I try to think that all of this is a bad dream. I almost persuade myself, as I sometimes do in nightmares, that if I can make myself fall asleep in the dream I will awaken outside of it. But this cannot be a nightmare. It is too prolonged, and the background sounds I hear, the murmuring of the brook, singing of sparrows and chestnut-sided warblers, the alders I grasp, the notes I set down, are all too real. My ever-searching eyes have always wanted to see, so keenly wanted to see, and to see so keenly. Now they do not want to look, do not want to find.

As I continue in my notebook—for the first time this year moving into shade to write—I hear the rustle of what can only be a wood turtle on the move. I can't make out exactly where the on-and-off rustling comes from. The wind has come up and surges in the pines, as though the day would change its mind about spring. Then I see movements not of the wind's doing in some fallen fern shafts. A young wood turtle appears, leaving his basking place—where I never saw him—probably because pine shadows have overtaken the stream bank in the past half hour and it is cooling down. He is hardly two feet from where I stand, on the other side of an alder mound on which I have set my vest in order to write. He is within a yard of the water's edge. I can see only his left front foot. But when I pick him up I find that he is completely whole, a perfect turtle. For two decades, most of the wood turtles I have recorded have been free of predatory damage. Now that rule has, in the turning of a single season, become the exception.

Seeing this six-year-old turtle, one I have come upon every year since I documented him as a hatchling, breaks the steady toll the day has taken on me. Unsure of when I will be able to come back to a reality I know I must face up to, I let this be my last turtle of the day. When have I ever walked away from such an April day, let alone the day of the wood turtles' first emergence onto the stream banks?

"It will never be the same here," I all but say aloud, the

thought racing through my mind as I pass through a tangle of raspberry, dense even though leafless and with new canes not yet risen. "Never the same" keeps repeating as I think of the intact, vigorous wood turtles I have seen in this forbidding cover and the adjacent sprawl of sweet fern, blackberry, and deer-tongue grass under a canopy of staghorn sumac and gray birch. I could hardly point to a single place where I have not seen an intact turtle in past seasons. The images of the dead first turtle of the year and today's wounded ones are gradually supplanted by that of the perfect six-year-old emerging from cover. (I suppress for now the ecological reality that he will have to survive another fourteen years to become a breeding adult.) I expand my thought: "Never the same—in my lifetime." The status of the colony that I have known here—with its abundance of unmarred young as well as adult turtles—cannot be reestablished within that limited time frame. But there is time here; it is part of the habitat.

I see more clearly than ever the dimensions of time and space that are required for, and have been the history of, such workings: the need for a stream entire, linked with another and connected to a river beyond, and all the spaces in between, a sizable enough fragment of the vast way it was only four centuries ago, when there was one continental landscape, and everything in it was interconnected with everything else. The race of humans who came here and supplanted the first of their kind to migrate here, who were not in essence landscape-takers, began a taking and disconnecting that has become an ever-expanding constant, a ceaseless marginalization and even eradication of ecologies in the ultimately impossible drive to satisfy human exigencies and desires, a drive exacerbated to the point of no return by overpopulation. The species that came to invent wealth created poverty, for its own kind as well as for the natural landscape. In wealth and poverty alike the human species now impoverishes the planet.

The wood turtles have time that I do not have. The brook trout, alders, otters, water . . . this system, an ecosystem, has time. If it can be left as an extended, untrammeled landscape, this colony of wood turtles will regain its former robustness. If the landscape is put into human service—I could say human servitude—and this is the global imperative of the day, the time of all these things will come to an end.

IN MEMORY ONLY

THAT BREATH of air just now, breathed back to me from the heated stream bank, the scent of sun on earth rising on the slightest stirring of the air . . . the mingled scents of moss and leaves, the brook. I remember and am there again, in that place that no longer exists, as a young boy who no longer exists. April's alchemy creates a memory out of mud and water, sunlight and fallen leaves; spring breathes on these and brings something not just to light but to life. At such unbidden moments, and they are fleeting, fragments of memory become so vivid that they live. I cannot see them, I can only feel them, these unconscious rememberings not just of what I was then but of what was all around me. That light of some deep yesterday, the sunlight on the water, the stream that sparkled by, the frog that looked back at me, and at the same time all the world around. Are these some last earthly existences destined to die with me? How is it they return to me, to take me back? Is there ever a going back to stay? Does all this lie in memory only?

FOLLOWING THE WATER

That flowing water! My mind wanders across it.
That broad water! My mind wanders across it.
That old age water! That flowing water! My mind
    wanders across it.

— *"Myth of the Mountaintop Way," Navajo poem*

RAIN UPON RAIN at the outset of April, spits of snow,
slants of sleet; the season advances with warm rains, then
holds in place with snow squalls and cold downpours, drisk,
and drizzle. But spring does not turn back. It moves on with
Earth's shift to that more favorable inclination toward the
sun and increasing increments of light, a planet turning in
its circumscribed track in space, its reined revolving within
a yearly circling of the star it travels with, constant for a

time in the cosmos. Snowmelt from winter's final caches, held in the prolonged cold embrace of hemlock stands and north-facing slopes, joins the runoff of rain. The earth is saturated. Not even the evaporation brought about by April breezes and the heavy uptake by bud-swelling plants can diminish the water. Upland hills that will be leaf-rustlingly dry by the summer solstice are so sodden that they could nearly pass for swamps.

Water is on the move, not only in the ever-flowing cuts and channels of perennial streams and rivers but in flashing silver runs so ephemeral that they rarely come to life outside of this season of abundant rain. It seems these intermittent streams need to be fed hourly. Their sources will be the first to give out as the last of the melting snow is exhausted and the frequent rains of spring drop off. They will lie as waterless traces, their slender cuts among roots and rocks on the forest floor, lined with fallen leaves, implying the glimmering runs that will not return until autumn rains or something on the order of a hurricane's deluge springs them back to life for a late-season race. Everywhere traveling onward, water seeps through the soil and slides over the impermeable underlying bedrock. At this turning point in the year it appears willful and restless, seeking places in which to pool, only to escape and flow on, as though possessed of the same zugunruhe, the migratory restlessness that is so strong in animate life at thaw. Here, inland and earthbound, water appears intent upon finding its way back to the ocean, back to the clouds, the sources from which it came.

I enter the dense emergent thickets of silky dogwood, silky willow, winterberry, and alder, with song sparrows singing and swamp sparrows trilling, and wade to the sun-flooded southern end of the vernal pool to look in on the islandlike masses of wood-frog eggs. In clearest water I see developing tadpoles twitching in the transparent medium from which they will be born. On the verge of hatching, they too pulse with an eagerness to move on, an innate evolutionary impatience arising from the fact that their natal water will not be here forever. One might think, upon looking into the overflowing pool today, that there would never be a time without water here. Yet the drying out always does take place, and in some years it can come with surprising suddenness, dooming the tadpoles who must become frogs before the water is gone.

Nothing is stagnant in April. Even isolated catchments tremble, as though the water in them is anxious to leap back into the air. The pool's surface vibrates, its quivering tension shimmers with sunlight. Unable to contain its vernal bounty, this broad seasonal pond releases a gently murmuring spill at the lowest point in its rim, an overflow that presses on to lower-lying wetlands. In this shallow slide of water I encounter another stream, a living tide that moves against the flow. An upstream migration of mayfly larvae, a solid insect caravan uniformly five or six individuals wide, twists in a long column along the margins of the spillway. This determined procession has a single intent: to reach the pool that is divined to be at the source of this streamlet, the seasonal pond that will last long enough to allow their meta-morphosis into adult mayflies, with wings that will lift them from the water for their brief last lives in the air.

Larvae line each side of the outflow, hugging its borders, wriggling, undulating. They are sorted by size, with the smallest at the landward edge, the largest closest to the central stream, some cuts of which, though only an inch or two deep, are channeled into currents too swift for the larvae to swim against. At frequent intervals, both large and small individuals lose their hold in the navigable edgewaters and are swept back the way they came, until they curl against the edge again and find a lodging place from which to take up their arduous journey anew, falling into place in the up-stream-inching column with near-military precision. Insects and water travel their respective ways. Time and place are graphically measured in these two tides, one living, the other nonliving. They both appear to be possessed of destinies. Resolute, but so small—one quarter to three quarters of an inch—the dislodged larvae face significant setbacks; but there can be no turning back.

Though varying in size, all the larvae appear to be of the same species. They are generally the first living things I see moving in the frigid waters at the initial opening of the ice each year, when the division between ice and water is reduced to its finest point, a pinpoint in temperature, on one side of which is ice, on the other, water. A metamorphosis in the physical universe that has a profound influence on all living things on Earth takes place at this all but immeasurable dividing line. My first sightings of these living, streaming mayfly larvae often occur through windows of thinnest ice. In near-stationary backwaters or gentle drifts, they undulate through the water column. At this seasonal moment they have come to a common direction and advance along a watery labyrinth among the wetland niches that exists only during flood times. Living mats of larvae edge their way along lingering ice or wriggle up films of water so thin that they are no more than a glistening on the saturated earth.

Many of the larvae are intercepted by other seasonal migrants, returning red-winged blackbirds and their companion grackles, who know the times and places of such abundant prey. Robins, attuned to this insect phenomenon, become wading birds for a time and feed on the teeming larvae, which are compelled by the current to run a gauntlet of shallows that barely cover their backs. But they are legion. Enough of them will reach the pool to fill the air above and all around at their moment of metamorphosis, perhaps no more than two weeks away.

I take the water's course and go with the drift, with water

barely moving, running little races, or standing still for a time, as it threads over and pools upon the land. At spring flood, water is at its fullest capacity for connecting the varied elements of the wetland mosaic I wade each year. It unites compartments that will later become individual isolated pools or channels and wet meadows whose surface water will inevitably fall away as rainy spring gives way to droughty summer. The unifying water of flood season is the medium that links me with all wetland niches, serving as my entrance into the wetlandscape and my conduit through it, my guide to the places of the plants and animals living within it.

Following the water, I walk glimmering traces into a dense maze of alders, morning alders still silver-beaded with rain that fell in the night. They have yet to leaf out, but their lengthening maroon and gold tassels are one of my measures of the awakening season's progress. Little more than a surface film, the water in this alder carr is so shallow that I cannot truly say I wade it. Twenty-five feet into the alder thickets, the outlet from the great vernal pool joins an intermittent stream at its turning to the south after a long descent from a steep, boulder-studded hill to the east. The stream's life, like that of the seasonal pond, is timed to the abundance of rain and snow. Because it has its origins in a spring and because spring is the season of its most essential running, I call it Spring Brook.

I look down this avenue of water, one of the most familiar faces of April: a surface sheen of white clouds and blue sky, crowded all along its margins by alders and silky dogwood; a length of water alive with wavering lights and black snakings of reflected alder stems; a passage of thirty yards or so through screens of warm gray laced with linear reds, the near alder and dogwood, to where it becomes lost in the maroon-gray maze of farther thickets. I take the day and its water and follow them into the season. Moving eastward, I wade into the morning and begin to track the day in the face of the trajectory of the sun that measures its passing. I cannot help but see the entrance that lies before me as an invitation. It is existence as invitation, as an entrance into an existence opening up before my own. In the blur of the stream, the alders, and the sky, time itself becomes a blur and I go with water that leads back to the past, on to the future . . . timeless water.

For twenty-five years I have been coming here to follow this same route of springtime waters. This is hardly a geological time frame, but I marvel at the constancy I witness. The water returns to retrace and reclaim its longtime runnings, slow flood drifts, and poolings. The alders hold their place. Nearing their time of metamorphosis, migratory mayfly larvae move against the stream, down which many wood-frog tadpoles will soon travel. Upstream migrants that in the past few days have begun to return for the season of the vernal pool include green frogs, bullfrogs, and spotted turtles. Individual spotted turtles have been making spring pilgrimages up this watery corridor far longer than I have, some perhaps for a century. Their species has inhabited the channels and pools of this wetland system (fewer and fewer remain that are this extensive and interconnected) since the retreat of the glaciers that carved its topography in the landscape more than a millennium ago. I wonder just how many generations of these turtles have made the journey upstream to the vernal pool at spring's flood-rich awakening, then back downstream at summer's advent and the time of low water. When did that first traveler to follow the retreat of the glaciers—there had to have been a first—head blazed with orange, jet shell adorned with a constellation of bright yellow spots, move up this clear flow so new to the world? I think of such firsts, so incomprehensible. I do not like to think of lasts.

I pass a small chain of alder mounds a little higher than all the others, where every April wood anemones bow and bloom, reflected in the moats of clear water that accompany their flowering time. Like the vernal pools and so many seasonally flooded wetlands, this shrub swamp could appear somewhat tenuous, even transient. One could take an impression of impermanence from an overview of alder and sapling red maple and the comings and goings of its shallow water. And yet year after year the water returns, and the shrub carr persists. It is the water, however slight and seasonal, that shapes and keeps this wetland for its time.

At the confluence of the spill from the vernal pool and Spring Brook I come to the first of two depressions in which the water I follow expands and lingers before its eventual entrance into and dissolution in the broad wetland mosaic, an interspersion of wet meadows, fens, marshes, shrub swamps, and swamps along the stream's course. This marshy pool is only seven strides across, perhaps a foot deep, set on eight inches of gripping muck. This is too deep and wet even for alders and sensitive fern; the pool has been colonized by reed canary grass, its seeds washed down from the vernal pool or transported on the backs of turtles, frogs, and salamanders. Long, intensely green, wavering strands of filamentous algae fill the narrow cut of the central channel, which the seasonal flow evidently keeps free of the entrenching reed grass. The algae form thick mats throughout the grassy zones as well. This pool, too, is alive with mayfly larvae. Here, given a comparative ocean to navigate, they appear aimless in their swimming to and fro; but eventually, individually and collectively, they fall in line at the head of the pool and, intent upon some higher water, the great majority join the formal procession traveling against the current. Some stay here until their time of transformation—or is it later arrivals from downstream sources that I see emerge from this minute pond as winged adults, joining those who rise at the same hour from the vernal pool?

Over the seasons, certain days and times, not fixed dates on any human calendar, are my own holidays, constants within the season's variables: the Opening of the Water; the Migration of the Mayfly Larvae; the Return of the Red-winged Blackbirds; the Arrival of the Frogs and Salamanders; the Time of Spotted Turtles Migrating; the Dance of the Mayflies; and, tightly cued to this, the Return of the Tree Swallows . . . So many, the litany goes on throughout the sequence of the seasons, to times of departures and the Turning of the Red Maple Leaves; the First Thin Ice; First Snowfall; the Long Winter Quiet. These are my holy days, set in the calendar of the seasons. Though regulated by the sun and the moon and the spinning of Earth, they are not limited to any twenty-four-hour period; there is no affixing a number to them. I mark these times as I see them with a common denominator: "Again."

I move on with the water sliding by. It is only at this time of year, and only along this particular intermittent stream, that I literally follow the water. I must walk east into the sun, which makes it hard to see. And wading with the current stirs up obscuring clouds of mud that billow ahead of me. Although this is no swift current, it exceeds my deliberate pace, which is broken up by many lingering pauses. Almost invariably I plan my routes so that I go west and

Study of reed canary grass.

upcurrent in the morning, east and upcurrent in the afternoon. These routes greatly enhance my chances of seeing before being seen. But during this time of water moving everywhere, and migration, I make this downstream journey day after day. The season and my sense of place compel me to go the way the water flows—a sentiment reinforced by the likelihood that I will, more days than not, intercept a spotted turtle or two traveling toward me.

My eyes are challenged by the bright reflected light of the sun thrown off by the water. Overcast days are worse, even with the sun at my back, for the mirror of sky glare is constant from any angle. I tried wearing polarized sunglasses, but water and light, surface and interior depths, became even more confusing. And the smoky lenses put me at a remove from near and distant landscapes. Somehow even sparrows and warblers singing at my ear seemed farther away. I lost something of the immediacy of my own wading feet and felt as though I were traveling in a bus with tinted windows. I have difficulty with binoculars as well. Although they are necessary at times in order to make a specific turtle identification, my eyes do not take well to them, and I am seldom in a situation that grants long-range sightings anyway. In order to really see, I need unaided eyes.

Over the course of more than fifty years of wading wetlands, my eyes have become specialized, adapted to seeing into the water, penetrating its reflective surface, reading its interior depths and the mazes of vegetation within it, the leaf packs, branch tangles, mud, sand, cobble, and stone beneath. My artist wife, who often paints swamps and marshes, urges me to put more blue into my own watercolors of wetlands. I reply that when I look at water I never really see blue. Perhaps because I am nearly always in the water, not looking at it from above, I see black and white, amber-gold, bronze, and dark tea. Often I see no color at all, only transparency; I see the things within the water as though they were suspended in thin air.

One time when we were both looking into the grassy vernal pool in early spring, my wife remarked on the brilliant, intense blues on the water, made all the more blue by its framing of straw gold reed canary grass. At that point I suddenly saw the color, reflected bits of sky scattered about the pool. As I squinted to keep my focus on the surface I saw blue everywhere: a dazzling Byzantine mosaic of cobalt, lapis lazuli, cerulean, and ultramarine. After a while, though, I had to make a visual adjustment in order to see into the water again.

On another occasion, when I took my wife on a wade into the bewildering blendings of water and growth, reflections and penetrations of light, overhanging and submerged tangles and sprays of grass, sedge, and shrub, she found it virtually impossible to make out a pair of spotted turtles in courtship who were oblivious to us as they moved about at our feet.

"One rarely gets such a good look at them," I whispered. She said, "I would never find turtles."

In an atmosphere of warmth and light that is still new to the season, a remembered dream I get to relive one more time, I continue along Spring Brook. A soft sheen of sunlight, warm in color, warm to the feel, reflects from dry leaves strewn over wet earth and from the smooth or speckled bark of endless stems and branches. It is not sharply focused and blinding, like light off snow or water, but an ambient, mesmerizing glow. Here and there along the brook's low banks are vibrant accents of yellow-green where sphagnum moss fills wet hollows and creeps over sodden logs and hummocks. A striking emerald green moss cushions the footing of each red maple sapling. Silky dogwood branches streak the warm gray haze of other leafless shrubs with crimson and maroon. The floor of the alder carr is a sun-bleached blur of fawn, ocher, sienna, light purple-grays, and gray-greens. It is wonderfully exhausting to try to encompass these lights and colors, to search them, and all the while try to read the alternately transparent and sky-reflecting water that threads among them. Lodging myself among some sturdier alders that incline over the stream, I rest, waiting and watching.

The midday hour becomes silence and stillness. I slow

all the more into the day. I hear an animal chewing. With a gradual turning of my head I scan for the source of the only sound near me. Not more than half a dozen strides away, a snowshoe hare nips the tips of an evergreen sedge's glossy blades. Whiskers twitching, he works his lower jaw vigorously. Other than that he, too, is motionless. His fur, though still marked with patches of winter white, has almost entirely gone over to the earth tones of his summer coat. He is well suited to pass unnoticed in his surroundings. Without making a sound in the dry leaves, he hop-walks a few more yards and settles down to nibble the points of another long sedge. Behind me I hear another animal scratching himself, almost certainly another hare. I twist a bit to track this sound and make him out, hunkered down on the tawny-leaved floor of the alder carr, immobile, his eyes half closed. He looks for all the world to be daydreaming, a luxury one would think his hunted, scampering kind could rarely afford. It seems that spring holds even these quick-footed ones in its spell. On the verge of an explosive full awakening, the season drowses. I feel only half awake myself.

The hare's somnolent repose belies his alertness. His nose wriggles continually, his sides reveal his rapid breathing. His erect long ears never stop turning, scanning the four directions, listening to the world. No doubt these hares have been well aware of me and have tracked my passage down the brook. I wonder at what distance their ever-listening ears first detected my approach. I think my repeated passings here have made me a nonthreatening part of their world. They know my scents and sounds, my form; they are used to me, and as long as I keep to my familiar rounds at my customary unmenacing pace, they will be at ease having lunch and taking naps all but within my shadow. Neither one moves as I extricate myself from my leaning place in the alders and resume my walk.

The fertile fronds of the sensitive fern, suggestive of the buttoned tail ends of rattlesnakes, set loose clouds of spores as I brush through them in crossing a backwater pool, dusting the water with a rust-red coating. The ferns have not yet raised new foliage, but their fertile fronds stand throughout the intermittent stream's course, clearly delineating its route among the alders. Sensitive indeed, this fern is burned by the lightest touch of frost in autumn and is late to unfurl its new green croziers, lest it be caught by the late frosts of a northern spring. By late May I will wade a thigh-deep swath of this wetland fern, making the dwindling water beneath it all the harder to search.

In scanning a pool-like run of the brook, below a sparkling braid that plays over a narrows formed by buttressing roots of red maples gnarling out from both banks, I see the tranquil surface come to life. There are swirls and ripples, and then the surface becomes still once more. Another disturbance riffles the sheen of reflected sky. These are surely the movements of a spotted turtle. As clear and shallow as the water is here, the distance and angle make it impossible for me to see into it. A dark head, its face radiant orange, appears and disappears. I see a dark shape moving, bearing brilliant yellow spots. And now another, suddenly overtaking and heading off the first. I have come upon a pair of spotted turtles, travelers who are combining a spring migration with a courtship chase. They have no doubt been feeding along the way as well, at least until the male caught sight of the female and became oblivious to everything else.

The object of his attention appears interested only in feeding and proceeding upstream even as the male makes clear his own intent of intercepting her. These conflicting purposes slow the process considerably, but the journey continues. I once saw a merry band of four spotted turtles, two of each sex, on such a springtime migration-cum-courtship chase, and although it was a somewhat unruly procession, it seemed as if it should be accompanied by stately Renaissance dance music. This day's couple travels to the faint rippling murmur of the stream-braid and a nearly incessant sequence of songs coming up from redstarts, yellowthroats, and yellow warblers in the brook-side thickets. Whether or not they take time for a coupling, these turtles will be in the vernal pool before sunset.

I continue downstream along the nearly level run of this seasonal brook to the second ponding, which I call the

tussock sedge pool, for the cushionlike mounds of the sedges
that emerge from its deepest trough. This ten-by-thirty-
yard depression serves as a way station for me; it is one of
my signal watching places at the time of spring migrations
and is a halfway house for the spotted turtles as well. Although their ground or, I should say, water time here is generally brief, the pool is an important hiding, foraging, and
sometimes mating place for them. For a couple of weeks
out of the entire season I find the turtles here, sometimes
four or six in a day. I rarely see them here outside of this
narrow window.

As I do each time I come here, I survey this clearing in
the alder carr from behind an especially thick stand of northern arrow-wood and meadowsweet before moving out into
the open. Nothing catches my eye in the pool or its associ-
ated channels, where a spotted turtle could appear at any
moment. As my eyes drift beyond the water, scanning its
adjacent shrub thickets, they are arrested by a startling turtle
shape, so large that it is out of scale with any search-image
I had in looking over these very familiar surroundings. My
instantaneous thought is that I have discovered an old, top-
size wood turtle with a smooth-worn carapace. But then I
realize that this turtle's shell—high-domed and blue-black
in its soft reflective sheen—is too big to be anything other
than a Blanding's turtle.

Now and again I find the young of this species as I track

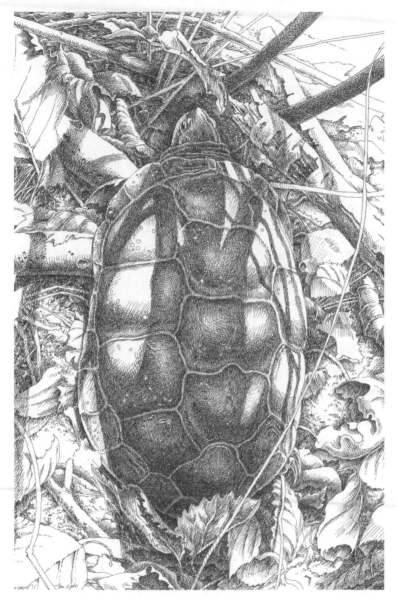

Blanding's turtle.

spotted turtles along this migratory route. Most are under twelve years old; I have never known an adult to travel this way. Even by the cryptic-behavior standards of most turtle species, Blanding's turtles move in mysterious ways, sometimes for miles, traveling overland, even traversing forested upland ridges where one would not expect to see a turtle, shifting among wetlands, with days spent in hiding without moving at all. Frogs scatter as I fight my way through restraining brush and deep-muck shallows. I cannot help but feel anxious upon making such a unique discovery, but I don't have to rush; there is nowhere for this turtle to go. She is terrestrial-basking several yards from any water or mud deep enough that she could elude me. At my first break toward her I see her lift her head slightly and look furtively left and right. Then she freezes. She too is aware that she has no place to go and can only attempt to go unnoticed. Wood turtles that I approach like this on land do not so much as blink an eye as I draw near and will rarely make a move at all unless I touch them. I slow my advance, then pause. I am in the extraordinary position of having an extended period of time in which to take in a sighting of one of these quick-to-disappear turtles. Sightings like this become indelible in my mind, yet in the excitement of the occasion—revelation, really—one can rush the moment and miss too many details.

The turtle's legs, tail, and long, long neck are withdrawn

into the helmetlike fortress of her nine-inch-long shell. Folds of her neck skin, as well as her head from just behind the eyes, protrude from her carapace. She faces the sun. Several small but distinct pits in her shell allow me to recognize her as an individual I have seen before, at least twice, the last time something like six years ago. We meet again. Many occasions are annual; others occur a number of times in a given year; still other meetings are separated by years or even a decade. Some occur once in a lifetime. With the long-lived turtles, my own life span will not allow for many future reunions; that is, if this place in its broadest extent is left to them, they will be here well beyond my time.

The turtle has oriented herself behind a clump of alder stems in such a way that several shadows of varying width drape over the contours of her shell. This alignment is probably deliberate; she is taking the afternoon's imperceptibly shifting shadows as a means of procrypsis, acquiring a disruptive pattern that helps break up the form of her shell and grant her a measure of concealment. Only when I run my hand lightly over the smooth, irresistible dome of her shell does she withdraw her head. Here, in the feel of this beautiful sun-warmed shell I have an extraordinary connecting with the season and the life that it bears. I leave her to her solarium and turn back to the tussock pool. Regrettably, my intrusion will break her bond with the day, with the April sun. That would have been so even if I had not placed my hand on her shell. When she feels it is safe to move she will return to the pool and hide for a time in one of its deepest, darkest recesses before continuing on a journey I wish I had a way of following.

I tend to linger where the water lingers; it is the middle of the afternoon and I am still by the tussock sedge pool. I stand on a broad crest formed by shrub mounds and strewn with windflowers, or wood anemones. Named for their trembling on any slight stirring of the air, the flowers are motionless in this still, still afternoon hour. My back is to the sun as I look into the black water of the pool's deepest trench from behind a screen of thickset winterberry stems, interwoven like some medieval fencing, my coign of vantage for looking over the pool. The profuse specklings of white lenticels on the submersed sections of alder and winterberry stems take on an amber cast in the tannic water. They mimic the patterns of a spotted or Blanding's turtle's shell and suggest one where there is none or conceal one who is there. Perhaps an example of ecology influencing development in a species, this kinship of carapace markings with the effect of the dark water and light lenticels characteristic of the woody wetland plants native to the turtles' prime habitats, or with the scattered sparks of sunlight, the forms and tones of seeds of sedges, grasses, and buttonbush, dropped in season and often persisting, hardly seems coincidental. Dark, tannic water, specks of sunlight coming through dense foliage, light tips on the "leaves" of sphagnum moss, seeds, circular pale pores on underwater stems—all these must have played a role in designing the shadowy blue-black, flecked, and spotted shells of these two turtles of kettle holes, fens, marshes, and swamps, the spotted and the Blanding's.

As I keep watch I sight another vigil-keeper. Waiting, watching, with a patient intensity and keen perception I would do well to emulate, a ribbon snake lies unmoving at my feet. Not having moved for some time myself (perhaps I can be more patient than the snake; I am not here for my daily bread), I have gone unnoticed by the snake I didn't see until just now. Waiting is a critical component of my observation, as it is of those I am most intent on observing. Most of the time, he who moves first is seen first. I have no idea when this silent one appeared. His stealth in approaching the pool has been so accomplished that he could just as well have slipped out from under my feet. His camouflage is remarkable, even by the standards of a world so infinitely, minutely, and resolutely dependent on crypsis. This bronzed, straw yellow, and shadow black ribbon of snake is wound over, under, and among a littering of leaves and twigs, coilings of fern, bleached vines, and strands of grass, all laced with ribbon snake–imitating weavings of sedge. Anytime I see a snake before he detects me and whips into motion, I take it as a reaffirmation of my interpretive eyesight.

Drifts of clouds that came together to take over the sky with the afternoon's advance have recently broken up and separated out. The sun is very hot. The snake's sun-struck sides expand and contract rapidly; he breathes at a hare's rate. With a barely perceptible flowing, disturbing nothing around him, he vanishes beneath a mat of fern wreckage. The silence of such animals in the upper layers of last year's fallen leaves, blades, and stems, so quickly brought to a rustling crispness, even on the soggy floor of the alder carr, by April's drying breezes, is as amazing as their endless ways of blending into virtual invisibility with their immediate surroundings. After several minutes the snake reappears, trailing his three yellow stripes over snaking alder roots, and slides into the pool. His fixed jet eyes fired with a spark of sunlight, his scarlet, black-tipped tongue flickering, he winds across an open stretch of dark water and weaves himself into the straw skirt of a tussock mound.

With a long leap and resounding splash a green frog simultaneously departs from the hummock. She had been statue-still while her protruding gold-ringed eyes took in the world around her. The legendary capacity of snakes for swallowing prey considerably larger than their heads notwithstanding, it seemed impossible that the slender snake could swallow such a large frog. But with the appearance of side-winding ripples on the surface of the pool and a slithering at the base of her sedge cushion, the green frog

Ribbon snake.

evidently did not care to calculate any of the finer measurings in nature and made her leap. Surely there is a long history of snake movements and their potential consequences encoded in the green frog's internal evolutionary guidebook. How far back in time does that history go, and how many pages does it have, inscribed with instinct?

During its flood season this tiny marsh, like any wild wetland, no matter what size, is a natural theater. It bears constant watching. There are intermissions, to be sure, but one act is soon followed by another in the script of the day, the scenes written sur le motif as they are performed. As the snake slips from view in front of me—I cherish such disappearances-before-my-very-eyes—a sudden sparkling of sunlight off broken water causes my head to turn toward a small spillway at the southeastern end of the pool. I have the best seat in the house, but this is a true theater in the round, and I cannot look everywhere at once. A male spotted turtle clambers up the cut through which water escapes and drops into the tussock sedge pool. In water as black as his shell he becomes a moving pattern of rows and scatterings of lemon yellow spots, as though he were a speeded-up film of a constellation sliding through a night sky. He glides among the upreaching winterberry, then tunnels under submarine sedge skirtings, where all his radiant markings vanish. He will travel on against the flow as I resume following it.

Over the first two seasons I came here, I never saw a turtle, even though, from my first looking in, I had the strongest feeling that this must be a spotted-turtle place, that these turtles must pass along this intermittent stream in their seasonal migrations to and from the vernal pool and must make some seasonal use of the tussock pool. But I was either too early or too late in my initial searches. And then, the first spring I found them, I saw eleven over three successive days. That was quite a revelation—if revelation can be anticipated, even expected. The turtles are far more transient than the water here and can easily be missed. But over time—I have needed time, and I have had it—I came to know the comings and goings of water and turtles in this place. At a certain hour on a given day, when the face of the season turns in the direction of migration, I sense that the turtles are on the move, and I come here to wait and watch.

The living and nonliving elements of the planet share a succession of synchronizations that are set within the variations of the passing seasons. They march to a single drummer. But the rhythms of the timing, which are attuned to the vagaries of climate, can vary by weeks from year to year. There is, on balance, in these cyclical variations a degree of constancy that allows me both the dream and the expectancy of appointments kept. They are crossings, intersections, in the arenas of minutes, hours, days . . . years. I endeavor to read the seasons, their cycles of water, light, temperature, and time, their at once constant and varying clock.

Repeated visits to the wetlands I am intimately familiar with, season after season, year after year, and the accumulated observations of all these wadings and walkings, have led to my developing something of a biological clock. Sometimes it is set so precisely to the moment in the season's progress that I can look up from my writing and drawing table to see clouds breaking up on an afternoon at thaw and know that the first wood turtle has left the overwintering stream to ascend a west-facing bank to take his or her first sun of the year. I go to a place on the stream bank and the turtle is there, sometimes one I have seen in that precise place, more often a different turtle responding to the same seasonal moment in the same riparian setting.

I leave the tussock sedge pool by way of the spillway through which the spotted turtle made his splashing entrance. Some migrants come to this pool via an outlet at its western end after making their way through a series of shallow channels and impoundments maintained by beavers. Some of the dammings and diversions of water that maintain this system are surprisingly small, secured at strategic points by packed branches and mud that elevate the surrounding water levels just enough to meet the beavers' requirements. When I look at one of these minimalist dams I cannot help but wonder at how a plugging of mud and woody debris a few inches high by a foot wide can be part of a scheme engineered to keep a broad impoundment in the permanent stream precisely at the level of the floor of a beaver lodge more than fifty yards away. All of these workings, of water on its own and water redirected by beavers, debris dams, natural levees, plant mounds, or deadfalls, provide passages and places for animals and plants. The interrelationships among water, earth, climate, plants, and animals are as good as endless over the space and time allotted to this mosaic of wild wetlands. Simply by virtue of being left alone, it becomes rarer with every passing day. My being here is inescapably colored by my profound awareness that its continuing to be left alone is by no means guaranteed. It is all but certain that the increasingly over-peopled world will find its way here, as happens in virtually all landscapes great and small on Earth, and will bend it to some human purpose, breaking its bond with time, countermanding its coevolutionary imperative, depleting its biodiversity, and erasing its remarkable natural history.

Sometimes I follow the water along the beaver channel and backwater wetlands that border the low-gradient, nearly level lowland run of the permanent stream about fifty yards to the west, which I call Alder Brook. It is one of the most difficult passages I make. Today I continue along my spring-flood route, which is not without its own challenges. A markedly uneven substrate that is at times solid, at times deeply mucky, and fencings and tangles of last year's fallen growth and intertwined woody shrubs, laced in places with thorny swamp rose, all make for slow going. As I follow the gently drifting water I thread my way out of the densely thicketed shrub carr and begin a gradual descent into a deepening depression in the topography that supports a fifty-acre mosaic of wet meadow, marsh, shrub swamp, red maple swamp, and widely scattered, deeper, permanently flooded pools. My watery pathway conducts me to a wide, fairly open swale of lake sedge. After bowing so often to the low arches of the alder carr, where the namesake shrubs grow horizontally as much as vertically, I am able to stand up and walk erect for a time.

The great depression in which this wetland complex is cradled will rarely be more flooded than it is today. Here are many waters, all linked to form one great water, with a bewildering array of plant assemblages and an abundance and diversity of animals. Some of the animals are resident, some come here daily (I would be one of these), and others pass through only once or twice a season. My clearly defined wading channel, little more than ankle-deep, becomes mid-shin-deep, then gradually knee-deep and deeper, all the while becoming more diffuse, so that a narrow streaming turns into a broad flood. Its progress is so impeded by persistent vegetation that the slow drift could appear to be a still-water marsh. Here Spring Brook loses its identity and becomes one with all other waters.

The day spreads out before me just as the water does. Thigh-deep now, I send out gently radiating ripples as I move into the marsh compartment. The water is at once amber-gold and clear, radiant with the fallen blue-joint reed grass that fills it, the persistent remains of last year's rampant growth in this emergent wetland. Above the water the sheen of sun-dried mats and sweeps of sedge and grass is nearly blinding. Already, spring green shafts pierce upward through the deep, densely matted layers of last year's blue-joint.

I wade on through a sea of sunken dead grass and new grass rising. An American bittern booms in the distance, from the same haunt in a wetland corner that gives rise to his pumping, wild, and rhythmic calls every spring. The return each year of a pair of bitterns to this same breeding place, hidden along the interface of an alder swamp and a thick wet meadow dominated by lake sedge and swamp milkweed, is as perennial as the flood and the rising of the reed grass. Not wishing to disturb these intensely reclusive birds, I stay well away from their nesting niche, content to be accompanied by their calls, one of the most compelling voices of the season. I can hear them from their home base even when I am in the vernal pool, a quarter of a mile away.

American bittern.

My tour along the current's lazy drift eases me from the grassy wracks of the blue-joint marsh into the deepening hollow of a tussock sedge marsh. Comparatively firm and uniform peaty turf gives way to mucky, uneven footing. Here the water drifts, lingers, or in riffling spills squeezes through narrow passages among the anchored, enduring sedge mounds.

In one of those niches that exist within broad colonies of established dominants, a deep-muck deposit that has built up between the blue-joint bed and the realm of the tussock sedge, several clumps of marsh marigold have found a perennial footing. Fully leafed out in rich spring green, they stand out among the bleached ocher and sienna that surround them. Already they are crowned with glossy, golden-yellow buds, highlighted with a few first flowers. These wetland wildflowers were called simply gold by early English poets. In their brightening of the chill early-season waters I wade, they are as good as gold to me. The *mari*-part of their common name may come from *mere,* an Anglo-Saxon word for marsh. It would not be out of place to call them marsh-gold.

In contrast with essentially all of the other growth throughout this wetland, whose persistent stems, leaves, blades, and in some cases seed heads allow some botanizing even in the heart of winter, all traces of the marsh marigolds disappear long before the coming of the frosts that end the growing season. Like the wood anemones, spring ephemerals that flower before the canopy of the alder carr shades them out, these succulent plants must complete their annual cycle of leafing out, flowering, and setting seed before they are overtopped by dense sprays of grass and sedge. Here in this tightly contested, tightly turfed realm, the marsh marigolds have not been able to proliferate into the extensive colonies they typically establish in the deep organic deposits and water regimes of seepage swamps and the muddy borders of woodland brooks. These same few gold-crowned plants arise each spring in this same place and stand as another landmark in my living map of the wet-lands. They are signposts of the turning of the season as well. When I come again to their bright green and gold, I know where I stand in place and time.

Or do I make too great a case for stasis? As I look at them, still thinking of persistence and perennialness, it occurs to me that the plants are smaller this year . . . there may be one less. It becomes clear that there are fewer flower buds, and I think back to a far more luxurious flowering crown of years past. I am aware now that these marsh marigolds are dying out, encroached upon by the expanding girth of the tussock mounds. These familiar golden lights of early spring will one day be extinguished by the plant succession that is a feature of all habitats.

The diminution of this signal flowering, which, as such

transitions generally are, has been gradual and had not clearly registered with me before. Some things one does not want to focus on, and in my nature there is a deep reluctance to face change. In critical areas of my own history, change has signaled loss. Two of my favorite words, as I wander the realm of the turtles, have been "same" and "again." I recognize the reality of transition, the necessity of flux. It is easier for me to think of cycles: the beaver dam cycle, the coming and going of glaciers. I sense that my ingrained mistrust of change rests largely on fear. "Things change," I heard as a small boy, grief-stricken from witnessing the annihilation of turtle places I had wandered and had so quickly come to love. This platitude was offered by way of remonstrance at my refusal to accept change and my railing against it—or, at best, proffered as ironic consolation. I have continued to hear that phrase all my life, as though it excused, compensated for, or gave some acceptable rationale for the havoc reaped in the name of "progress." Such mindless mantras, non sequiturs uttered in the guise of wisdom, allow people all too easily to overlook, and to forget, consequences. Love must never learn to live with loss, the destruction of a dream or a reality, the taking away that is so blithely passed off as change.

Five-thirty . . . the afternoon advances. The bittern calls again, *uh-WONK uh-tunk, uh-WONK uh-tunk,* in a generously repeated series, an evocation of the season that draws me more deeply into it. Over the passage of years the individual singers change, but the song of the bittern, as of the others who declare spring, remains the same. As long as I have been coming here, the place from which the bittern calls, the hidden nesting place possessed of its own roots, has remained the same. As long as the water keeps to its seasonal rounds—as long as it is left alone to keep them —this complex and enduring wetland system, with flux and cycle factored in, will maintain its domain, and a pair of bitterns will find their place to nest within it. Successive generations will remember and return to this watery complex, a pinpoint on the planet, from wintering places as far away as Mexico or Panama.

Spring is so much a season of remembering, of returning and greeting anew. The water remembers and returns, enlivening the landscape with light, sound, movement, and silent reflections as it retraces ancient courses and refills historic pools. I come back again to places from which I have been distanced by the forbidding cold of winter and its barricades of thick ice and deep snow, and by the indoor aspects of my life. I come as visitor-observer, more different from turtle and sedge than they are from one another, in terms of being of and in this place. But I come with links of continuity and connections that give me a sense of belonging that I need not fully understand. In many ways I feel that I come back from some great distance, some deep time, like a migrant bird or a turtle awakening from a half year's sleep within himself, from a being away that goes back even beyond my boyhood. Each year's wading makes the next year's all the more compelling. All I know is that I must come back. Once I have returned, being here is enough.

It is quarter past six as I turn among the tussock sedge mounds, wade from the deepening channel that leads to the dense tangles of another shrub swamp, and head to shallower water. I skirt the rustling tussocks and wade into the lasiocarpa meadow. I have named this marshy compartment after the species name for the graceful plant that fills it with sweeps of grasslike growth, *Carex lasiocarpa,* the woolly-fruited sedge. I am a little above knee-deep in water and waist-deep in the ethereal sedge. Virtually all of the growth around me consists of this plant. With long, trailing blades about one-twelfth of an inch in width, it has a deceptively delicate appearance. Under favorable conditions it establishes monocultures as unforgivingly exclusive to other growth as those of the taller, coarser lake sedge, cattails, and even the woody alders. New shafts reach six to nine inches above the water, lithe, sharp-pointed, spring green. Their reddened bases stand out sharply in the clear water.

This first emergent thrusting forth forms a watery field of erect spikes that will extend to form a sheening haze of long, arching twists and sprays that bow and sweep with every stirring in the air. When the sedges are at full growth, stronger winds create grassy waves in passing over them, as though the plants themselves were water. Last year's pale, flowing blades fill the water from the surface to the turfy substrate they have built up here. They have been arranged carefully: not a hair out of place, it seems, combed and brushed by the slow, swirling slide of the water.

And throughout these graceful arrangements of sedge are windings of large cranberry, the one plant that finds its place and even proliferates among them. Fruits from last autumn persist on the pliant lacings, which keep their leaves all year, deepening to dark maroon in winter and greening again in April. In most years the seasonal shallows that now inundate most of the cranberry vines are gone by summer solstice. While the water is here it provides another favored niche for spotted turtles.

I come again at this time of year to wade in the late light of day, to hear the bittern pumping and listen to the rain of twitterings that falls from tree swallows not long returned, as they wheel in the high open air above this great wetland depression a few final times before dark. Red-winged black-birds call—always there are red-winged blackbirds calling at this season, wherever I wade. The water is so open and clear now, at its greatest depth and with vegetation just be-ginning to come forth within it. The water magnifies, not only the strands of sedge, which seem to flow without

Spotted turtle in cranberry vine.

moving on while the flood drift moves through them, but also the day, the hour, the precise point in the season's passage. This great pooling of collected meltwaters and gathered rains intensifies the light within it, the light upon it, the light reflected from it. Here spring is magnified in clear water lying upon land. Even the calls of distant red-winged blackbirds seem magnified as they carry over the waters of wet meadows, marshes, and swamps.

I wade across this shallow sea of water and sedge to a channel that circles its southern rim. I don't know if it was water that originally cut this channel along the edge of a slight topographical elevation, which effectively divides acres of marsh from acres of shrub swamp, and then animals took to using it as a corridor, or if larger animals first walked this way to skirt the difficult emergent shrub thickets, wearing a trail into the substrate that water then followed and over time shaped to its own purpose. At any rate, I follow a route that water takes and that also serves as a wetland passage for moose and deer, muskrat, mink, starnosed moles, water shrews, spotted turtles, young snapping and Blanding's turtles, green frogs, and mayfly larvae.

I would like to see a list, reaching back to the time of the origins of this watercourse, of all the life that has passed through, lingered, or taken root here. Somewhere beneath the built-up muck and vegetation, there must be a record of the day when the last of the ice shelf turned into crystal-clear glacial meltwater running over sand, the day that initiated the return of life to the deglaciated Northeast. At thaw, as the last of the ice shelves drop from mounds of shrubs and royal ferns in clear-running, sand-bottomed channels, I have intimations of that momentous melting in scenes that seem reenactments of it in miniature. Perhaps not long after that glacial retreat—at least in a geologic time frame—members of my own species, early enough arrivals to be called indigenous (though so much later in coming here than the preglacial turtles and ferns), followed this very route on hunting sojourns or seasonal migrations, without the comfort of insulated waders.

I suspect that it is a combination of treading feet and seasonally drifting water that keeps this channel open, a slender conduit little more than a foot and a half wide over most of its gently snaking length. It divides further as it links networks of other channels and pools throughout the marsh and swamp elements at the eastern and western extremities of the complex. Many of the watery cuts are so narrow that I can barely slip one leg past the other in wading through. As with the intermittent stream, the water finds its varied ways here, flood time after flood time, to reclaim its runnings and pondings and so define the enduring wetlands. For several decades now I have been one of the animal forces that helps keep the channels open, as I repeatedly retrace their labyrinthine networks.

Even in this leafless early flood season I see a brushy haze of dense thickets and crowding screens of shrubs when I look directly ahead. I could almost forget that I am in a wetland, and nearly half immersed at that.

The depression within a depression in which this shrub swamp is set combines the deepest—though rarely exceeding thirty inches even at times of highest flooding—and most permanent water with the densest growth to be found in the overall wetland complex. The shrub swamp is also the site of the earliest ice-out and thus it is the citadel of overwintering spotted turtles. I call it the Tangle, although any guest I brought here might observe that any of the surrounding interspersions of shrub swamp and marsh is every bit as much a tangle.

I have come here over the seasons of so many years, from March or April's opening of the water until October or November's closing over, that I have developed something of a spotted turtle's familiarity with the labyrinthine landscape. My feet, even through waders and wading shoes, have acquired a very literal feel for its watery pathways and the vagaries of its substrate. I get a few reminders each year, as I rediscover hidden depths of muck with a sudden unexpected sinking. My passage here is perhaps not typical wading, for I must knee my way among unyielding mounds of mingled shrubs, royal ferns, and sedges and shoulder my way through alders. Moving through the Tangle is a total-body experience.

Though I know this wetland so well, in its purely physical as well as its ecological and metaphysical aspects, neither the familiarity nor the hardships breed contempt. Being here has brought me to a knowledge, both tangible and ineffable, of a world apart, completely distinct, from that of my own kind. How many of us, and how often, think of the fact that we live our time on a planet, within that planet's time? What good is it to be alive on Earth and never come to know at least the place where one lives? We don't even try to know it with our senses, much less with our minds and spirits. How many human feet in the industrialized world know anything more than floors, pavement, lawn, or manicured sandy beach in a lifetime? We live on Earth without walking it. What do we touch with our hands? So many human eyes and ears see only the human-constructed landscape, hear only human sounds. Wild hills and swamps are looked at casually, if at all, viewed as little more than a backdrop for human dramas. So many voices, so many languages beyond human tongues, are never listened to. We are in fact overwhelmingly out of our senses. Our eyes are open for such a brief time, our appearance on Earth between two unfathomable sleeps. Are we to sleepwalk through it?

I edge my way out of the Tangle's final snarls. In snagging my sweater and catching my hair, the alders, winterberry, and swamp rose seem intent on keeping me here. Late in a long, slow day of wading I settle into a thigh-deep pocket, most of it mud, among the alders. I haven't the energy to immediately struggle out; it is one of those occasions when I am just as happy to be held in one place for a time. I am not far from the water's outermost curling, as it turns in a shallow arc along what might appear to be the upland border. But the wetlands extend beyond the margins of this shimmering slide of visible water. On the far side of the alder carr that has detained me rises a swamp composed not of shrub thickets but of trees, a red maple swamp. The trees are radiant in the last lingering slants of sunlight that play across their forty-foot crowns.

A flock of common grackles settles noisily into the high red maple canopy, each one a jet black bird silhouette distinct in the smoky blur of upper branches and the crowning glow of red-sienna twig tips, bright red buds, and flowers. Swamp sparrows continue their flitting and calling in the alder and royal fern mounds darkening around me. Water glides by in a silent sheet, brightening as the alders go black. Bound for lower ground, it swirls away from the upland ascents, its surface a constant quivering of tiny braids and voiceless riffles—alive and ever moving at the springing of the year. Here I will turn away from the water, which moves on among the alders, a broad silver slide finding its way to the permanent stream.

In its final run this lowland drift is channeled into a network of deeper cuts through belts of alder on wetland plateaus, sharply defined races banked by unyielding root and turf. Here the constricted runnings become forceful enough to keep their courses clear of sediments, cutting down to underlying sand. As the great depression slopes downward to its lowest point, the bed of Alder Brook, water quickens in these sluiceways and takes on the voice of a babbling brook, as though eager to get on with the race to the greater stream.

As daylight diminishes, the peep-frog chorus intensifies in the backwaters of a fen a quarter mile away. With raucous clamor and a rushing wind of wing beats a flurry of grackles lifts off from the topmost canopy of the red maple swamp. In the quieting that follows, I hear again the drift of evensong from their red-winged cousins on the far side of the wetland mosaic. The season, like the water glimmering all around, extends before me.

A DAY IN THE
SHADOW OF A PINE

Junto a las aguas quietas
Sueño y pienso que vivo.
[By quiet waters
I dream and think that I live.]
— *Luis Cernuda*

19 APRIL. I touch the morning sun where it touches the furrowed and plated bark of the pine. Sunlight finds its way through the tree's dense crown to warm the trunk and enhance its resinous scent. Sun warms the color as well, shifting small illuminations, washes of gold over lavender-gray here and there in the prevailing cool, deeper violet cast of white pine bark in shadow. How many suns are there in the

day? Sunrise, morning sun, the sun at its zenith, afternoon sun, sunset, and all those intermediate points. There is a sun for every season and all gradations of them. This pine has not yet attained half its potential girth and height, but still the sun of nearly a century's seasons has played over its bluish green crown, marking the turnings of all those days.

Touching trees has always grounded me. Before I knew their names I knew them by their feel, by the colors and textures of their leaves and bark, the ground on which they stood. As I spent nearly all my time in turtle places, the trees I touched were mostly those of swamps. In the same way I came to know the shrubs, more numerous and diverse, which my hands were constantly gripping for a necessary physical steadying, as well as for other groundings. Trees and shrubs were something to take hold of in an insubstantial world, something to provide me rootings and something by which to take root. In time I came to know the names they had been given. I couldn't get enough of learning their names, common and scientific and eventually even in the foreign languages I studied.

Black bears mark trees, rubbing, biting, and clawing them to designate their territories. I touch trees, my signal trees, most of them sentinels marking points where I enter or depart from a marsh or swamp. I touch them at each coming and going throughout the seasons. When I can reach a shaft of sunlight striking a tree's bark, I place my hand there.

Other trees mark a place along the way in my wetland circuits. At the same time they mark a station in the seasons. Some I touch day after day for weeks on end, others but once in several years. Some I have touched only once in decades; some I will never touch again because they have been taken away or because I cannot bear to go back to where they stand. Storms and lightning have taken some — there is no loss in this.

I am in the quiet here, the silent now of this slowly moving shadow. Time stays with me awhile. There is always a sense of returning for me in such a place. I come back again to tree bark and shadow, intervals of bird song and silence, the voice of the wind, the streamlet in its silent slipping by . . . back to a day in the swamp in boyhood when I had a sense in the present of a day in some deep past. I enter a confusion of time that allows not a better understanding of time, but a deeper relationship with it.

There are no empty hours in these wild places, no unit of time in which nothing happens. There are durations in which it might appear that nothing has changed. But something is always taking place. For how long now have I observed no more than the shadow of the pine in its incremental shifting as constant, if not as continually observable, as the glimmering water drifting by? There is the invisible passage of time, revealed by the sundial of this white pine. I am so aware of this place, this crossroads of life and the seasons, as a theater of time. There is as much time coming as passing . . . it flows over me as the nearby water flows over a fallen alder stem or as the pine tree's shadow moves over the earth. Do I dream the day or experience it? Watch it go by or go with it?

I come here during the spotted turtles' migrations, the season of so many returnings, to stand by this sentinel tree and watch the season for a while. When the turtle migrations end, I leave the pine to the rest of the year. Whenever I am here or in any of the places I am this deeply drawn to, I feel a connectedness, a filling in of some profound, vague emptiness. I need to be empty of all distractions. I come to forget and to remember.

Since early boyhood there have been two foundations: to be there and to return. I feel again that promise kept, kept from the day of the first turtle, those first few hours of being there. I come also to know where to be. The places have changed as landscapes have been ground under, but it is all there waiting in the places that remain. All that opened up to me in that first place, the intuitive revelations and empirical observations, holds on in this place that has been left to the workings of nature—where, for want of a better word, "wildness" lingers on.

I come to meet the day, and the day comes to me. I am here not to gather information but to receive information; to breathe in and out the pine-scented air, take in the nourishing silence, listen to the wind, the birds, the frogs; to watch the water shimmering by and regard the slow turning of the shadow of the pine as it marks the moving day. There is recording and there is experiencing. On some occasions I make notes, but today I transcribe nothing. There is that which cannot be transcribed, cannot be set down or held in any way. I can bear witness, but I cannot truly catch the April light, the wind, the water, or in any real way capture the turtle who passes by, take hold of the frog chorus . . . the immersion is intangible, the experience ineffable. It is like making love. I can only wait for it to circle back and go again to meet it. It is making love.

I stand in one of those places where I can see the world devoid of human presence, my own species gone entirely. In sunlight and by moonlight the shadow of the pine would continue for its time to wheel in its slow seasonal circles. The wind would be the same, the water streaming by. The ever-indifferent seasons would follow their course. The profoundly heavy burden of the global human footprint would be absorbed. The deep disruption of what was here before *Homo sapiens* and of what might have been without our species' appearance would be forgotten in the ongoing. The sun, the moon, and the stars would notice nothing. No god would grieve. There would be a return to an ancient silence.

A snake's head rises from dead leaves and dried sedge: slender head, slender neck, jet eye set with sunlight. His black-tipped scarlet tongue flickers; the rest of him is as still as a stick. Then there is a rhythmic swaying from side to side, his head fixed on a neck held stiff, and then a slow bobbing of the head as the swaying continues, followed by a fluid pouring of life taut in snakeskin, a magic movement with no outward sign of how it is achieved, as though water had become reptile and could flow independently of gravity. A garter snake trails himself among twistings of running swamp blackberry to a frozen-rope spell, his anterior fourth upright, head leveled horizontally.

A catbird's call and a brief, solitary piping from a peep frog is followed by the almost whispered trill of a gray treefrog. The wind that talks in trees speaks pine in my ear. The mingled twittering of warblers and emphatic calls of a yellowthroat come closer, almost to my very shoulder, as my stillness endures. The snake has not moved in seven minutes. The intentness of his gleaming eye—no tongue flicking now—seems pure listening. The wind whispers at times in dry leaves, but I hear it mainly in the high trees, soughing in the pine, swishing in red maple canopies just flowering, not yet leafed out. The snake curls in a graceful arc and slips out of sight beneath fallen leaves and branches.

Above the fawn of fallen leaves, journal pages from last year's seasons scattered about, pressed down by months of snow for the spring sun to open and read, dull green begins to replace the wine reds and deep maroons of winter in the

Studies of a yellowthroat.

perennial leaves of the running swamp blackberry vines.
My left hand reaches out and holds a gray birch sapling,
slowly rotating on its agreeable chalky warmth and slender, satisfyingly geometric roundness.

To move with a day as a shadow passes over the earth,
to breathe at the pace of its passing . . . I give my shadow

to the pine's; at intervals cloud shadows take both of ours away. In the pine shadow's outer arc, shade dances away at times and the sun's warmth splashes upon me. Against the trunk I am in the cool heart of the shadow. As the afternoon lengthens, the pine tree's shady silhouette comes to fit almost exactly over the tussock sedge pool, all but its easternmost end. A strong wind has come up and fairly roars in the treetops, gently rocking the winterberry from time to time. The day begins to slip away. I think, at times, of loves other than landscapes.

TRANSFORMATION

FOLLOWING WHAT appears to be an endless caravan of mayfly larvae swimming against the flow, a teeming migration departing from a scroll pond in the floodplain, I track my way up the little brook they are ascending. The streamlet has cut a narrow draw, down to stones, in a steep, forested slope that rises from the floodplain. Like most of the feeds to this serpentine coastal-plain river, this little brook appears to be seasonal. Two curiosities lead me on: where does the water come from, and where are these mayflies-to-be going? It is always intriguing to see where such a streaming issues from the earth, where it appears from subterranean runs to sparkle in the shifting lights of the forest and run silver and black in its shadows, enlivening the landscape with movement and, in spills here and there along its rocky descent, with murmurings and music. I am also drawn by the possibility, which rarely proves to be the case, that this slender springtime run emanates from a wetland large enough to support spotted or Blanding's turtles in the upland woods.

I am familiar with the migrations of mayfly larvae making their way against the drift of water throughout the gradually sloping wetlands, where they are emblematic of my first followings of water in a new season. Ascending from this farther floodplain later in the season, these larvae are quite likely a different species from the one I am so familiar with —it is not easy to make a definite identification of any one species of the 676 known to inhabit North America. These larval insects move with a determination and intimation of destiny that would seem more the province of spawning salmon. Minute bits of driven life, a living seasonal tide that is timed to move against a temporal streaming of water, they press on, swimming with their characteristic undulations, ceaseless, untiring. They are one of the inexhaustible living energies powered by an exceedingly minimal energy base, in this case bits of algae and decaying leaves. They will not be deterred by surges or tumbles of water in the uneven terrain or by debris dams of twigs and sodden leaves. In some level terraces along the run there are pools just deep and broad enough to harbor little green frogs and bullfrogs; they keep to outlying areas or headwaters in order to avoid larger members of their kind, who would make no distinction between them and anything else in their diet. How long is this column of larvae? It has lined the entire length of the draw along which I have walked, a distance of nearly half a mile. I did not join the procession at its beginning, but perhaps I can follow it to its end.

At length I do come to the end of my search, that is to say, to the beginning of the water. And here, too, the journey of the mayfly larvae has its end. The water's origin here is not a sphagnum-moss seep or rocky spring but a shallow shrub-swamp pool, thick with emergent winterberry. At times of abundant snowmelt or rain, groundwater wells to the surface at this interface, recharging a wetland basin high in the hills, filling it to the brim and over the brim, from which it flows on to follow the cut it has been carving in the landscape since the melting of the glaciers, down to the floodplain, for a final meander to join the river.

The pool teems with larvae. The air is filled with mayflies rising, pale-winged insects trailing long filaments, like tiny kites with three tails. I arrive at the site, and the moment, of a stunning transformation. As larvae continue to stream into the pool, subimagoes, as the mayflies transitional between larvae and adults are known, depart from it. They take to the air and fly short distances to alight on twigs and branches, where they will wait one more day for their final transition. At its culmination they shed one last skin, this time with delicate wing coverings, to go forth as fully formed adults, or imagoes.

Following this, one act of life remains: mating. They will not be feeding; in fact, they have no mouth parts. The males, great numbers of them, will unite in a swarm, filling the air above the pool and beyond, to perform a dance that may not last a day. The males of each species choreograph a unique aerial ballet, a synchronization of vertical and horizontal movements, cued to a certain time of day. The females of their kind recognize the visual and temporal pattern and fly into the swarm, where they are quickly seized by males. Immediately after mating, the females descend to the water to lay their eggs. All, males and females alike, die following this coupling in the air. A life of perhaps a year (two or three years in some species) as egg and larva ends in as little as several hours or one day of adulthood. The temporality that marks their order has led scientists to name it Ephemeroptera. They have their "day of wings," one might say, as the term is derived from the Greek *ephemeros,* lasting a day, and *ptera,* wings.

I have seen the migrations of larvae and the winged dances of adults throughout my familiar wetlands over the course of many years, but I have never before witnessed this moment of metamorphosis. I look intently at the swimming larvae and the subimagoes ascending from the dark surface. In a fraction of a second the split skin of a former life is left behind for that brief time in the air. I try to make out the actual dividing line, the instant of the aerial insect's emergence from the husk of the aquatic, gill-breathing larva. This is not the long-drawn-out, laborious work of a dragonfly extricating itself from the exoskeleton of a nymph. I follow some larvae as they rise to the surface and see them as they touch it, but I cannot see the actual departure: one moment there is a larva with its back just breaking the water, the next a mayfly in the air, with the shed skin floating below. Transformations, dividing lines—is there any greater metamorphosis, any narrower dividing line, than that of the invisible instant separating life and death?

Frogs are abundant and active throughout the pool, catching mayflies as they rise into the air or struggle upward through mazes of overhanging branches and sedges. A hermit thrush works the shoreline, snatching up larvae before they transform. This woodland bird becomes a wading bird, albeit in mere films of water. I have seen robins, red-winged blackbirds, and grackles, who know precisely the places and timings of these migrations, pursue larvae in this way each spring at the overflow of the vernal pool. Perhaps one thing that guides these long migrations is an adaptation to move to fishless waters for this elemental, vulnerable metamorphosis. But I see nothing that I could interpret as

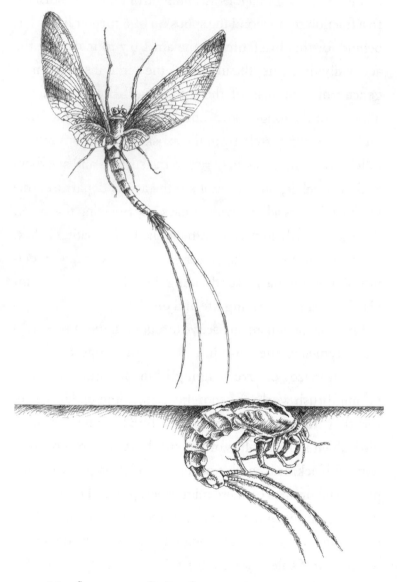

Mayfly metamorphosis.

an effort to elude predators; nothing in this critical timing allows for delay or avoidance. It is not about the individual but about a species en masse, as one identity: numbers plotted against a common fate. In this communal going forth lies the persistence of an ancient order of life.

GRAY TREEFROGS

27 MAY. A welcome new voice, one that I have been anticipating for some days now, breaks out as I wade the swale. After the first choruses of wood frogs and peep frogs herald spring's arrival, these loud trills of the gray treefrogs signal the season's steady progression toward summer. As is typical of their intermittent, infrequent daytime vocalizing, the treefrog chorus comes up all at once from hidden places in the emergent shrub borders and occasional islands of shrubs and saplings in this great, grassy vernal pool. It rings out for three or four minutes, then suddenly drops off to silence. I make one of my annual notations: "Hear first gray treefrogs."

Having no proper voice of my own to celebrate the seasons—I am as silent as the turtles in my wanderings—I am happy to have the calls of frogs, songs of birds, sounds of wind and water, to serve as my expressions. I love being silent as much as I love being in the silence, that is, of being where there is no human noise for some periods of time. (There is no lasting freedom from human sounds, but even a minute is sweet and healing.) Here are only the voices of nature and at times no sounds at all. In time another chorus erupts and rises up all at once, as though on cue from some conductor invisible to me but seen by dozens of frogs in their scattered hiding places. What baton is raised to set them all singing at the same instant? They fill the mild May afternoon with their vibrant trilling and then, as though the baton has been brought down, end their chorus as abruptly as they began it. This one communal voice of the many has always mystified me. Silence takes over again, above the still water lying beneath leisurely white drifts of cumulus clouds, soft in the sky with their blurred edges.

About to wade on, I hold still, arrested by a thought: "Hold on . . . these frogs are here, all around me." Although by day they sound like—and evidently I have been content to regard them as—disembodied voices, spirits and sprites, phantoms of spring who come to life by night, the frogs do exist in the physical universe. There are no large trees with great cavities and sloughs of bark in this seasonally flooded wetland; it doesn't seem possible that all of these frogs can be completely hidden from sight.

I have gone out to look for them by flashlight when they take up their all-night chorusing with resounding enthusiasm. Such searches in pitch-black darkness in the shrub swamps that these frogs favor for breeding have always been quite difficult. Some, such as rhodora, buttonbush, or blueberry swamps, are all but impenetrable and often complicated by treacherously deep, mucky, boglike substrates. At times I have had to suddenly grab hold of branches and stems to keep from going under in deep sinkholes. This is an alarming enough experience in broad daylight, let alone by night.

As is the case with spring peepers, it is nearly impossible to pick out the call of an individual treefrog from the deafening many, and all the more difficult to track the call to the frog who sings it out. Gray treefrogs are good ventriloquists, their loud trills seeming to come from anywhere and everywhere—everywhere but where they are. Encounters with them outside of their several-week-long breeding season, when they have departed from the wetlands and dispersed through the upland forests, are uncommon chance events. In boyhood, one of the rare places I could count on finding them away from their breeding pools was above the treetops, on a water tower I climbed, with barely suppressed terror, in games with friends.

As a consequence of my avid turtle focus, my eyes are virtually always on the water. I can miss an entire day's sky except for its reflections on the waters I wade. Now, with a new quest in mind I look upward. I let my eyesight ascend trunks and stems, then move along horizontal branches, trying to penetrate mazes of woody forkings and criss-crossings, layers and layers of leaves; my eyes become treefrogs looking for treefrogs. With nothing specific to go by, save that I do know what these frogs look like, I keep my head tilted to the canopy. I find it even more awkward to wade looking up than looking down. From all my years of looking for turtles, I have become something of a specialized animal, one with a neck permanently inclined to the water and ground at my feet.

Some friends who conduct fieldwork with birds once told me that they are often in wetlands and yet never see turtles. A group asked me to guide a tour and give them pointers on how to look for them. Lesson number one proved quite basic. After fifteen minutes or so I looked up to see them all with heads skyward, eyes affixed to binoculars. Those who observe birds are obviously accustomed to seeing what they seek considerably more frequently than those who look for turtles. "You won't find turtles in trees," I called out to them. But then, many of my bird sightings have come by way of a reflection on the water.

Head tilted up, I let my eyes do most of the moving; I

take a stride or two and scan my surroundings. This is how I look for turtles, but with my head inclined to the water or the earth rather than the canopy. And in considerably less time than is entailed in searching for something new to me, perhaps within seven minutes, I see a treefrog. Whether, as on some uncommon and fortuitous occasions, I find what I am seeking almost immediately, or whether it happens only after long searchings, sometimes over several seasons, there is something sudden and startling about finding the sought-after. The two-and-a-quarter-inch frog is settled into the narrow crotch of a nearly perpendicular forking upreach of winterberry holly, in a welter of vertical and horizontal branches. Mimicking the color and pattern of winterberry bark, he has become one with his embracing surroundings. He appears to have inflated himself somewhat in order to leave no froglike outline, to become an indistinguishable part of the whole. Loose folds of skin obscure what might be the revealing contour of a leg. In a group of animals known for their crypsis in color, pattern, and motionless-ness, the gray treefrog is legendary. He doesn't move as I approach and look at him closely from different angles, even when I move some slender branches in order to get a photo of him.

With several strides and turnings of my head I see an-other. This is how it is: one must find a treefrog (or wood turtle or any of the other most hidden ones) before one can find a treefrog. This one is on a dead branch arching from a dying elm sapling at the edge of the alder-winterberry border that rings the large, open central zone of reed canary grass and tussock sedge in this vernal pool, which is unusual in its wetland class for its size and its abundant and varied vegetation. Here the treefrog quite successfully passes himself off as one of the knobs and branch stubs of the stressed elm. I am reminded of musk turtles who mimic bumps on logs when they climb riverine deadfalls to bask; the head and legs hang down, pressed against the log, and the knoblike dome of the shell very closely approximates a branch stub.

My third frog is not so well hidden, perched on a horizontal stem of winterberry in a setting with a more open canopy, about four feet above my head. With his front legs tucked under his chin and his feet curled into fists, he looks down on me with the insouciance of the Cheshire cat. His bower is crowded with leaves, through which the strong sunlight passes, and he has taken on the green cast of his glowing ambiance. This chameleon-like adaptation produces at times rather green gray treefrogs. As I look up at him I am struck by the thought that these frogs have been watching me for years and also by the humbling realization that I, with my reputation for being an especially keen observer of nature, have been wading this seasonal wetland from thaw until it dries up in midsummer for three decades, and it has not occurred to me until today to try for a day-time sighting of one of these tree-dwelling amphibians. From the angle of one's eyes to the focus of one's mind, one can never have enough ways of seeing. And no matter how hard we look, however much we see, there is inevitably much that goes unseen.

My fascination with this game-cum-challenge of finding the treefrog in the swale leads me to make out the most cryptic one yet. He is settled in a small hollow at the branching base of a red maple. Anything recognizable as part of a frog is all but lost in the confusion of color, pattern, texture, and scrambled outlines of scaly tree bark layered with lichen.

Gray treefrog.

Bark and lichen are as much a part of this frog's ecology as woodland and wetland. I record him in my notebook as "lichen with eyes." I impress myself with this discovery. It is always reassuring to find that my eyes can still do such work, make such interpretations. It is largely a visual language that I endeavor to read in the wetlands and their surroundings.

The frog does not blink as I bend over him for a close-up photo, shifting my camera around, almost in his face. I wonder at what point he would consider that danger—or even death itself—was so imminent that he would make a leap for it. Although I am loath to cause any disturbance, my curiosity, which I suppose I could justify as a scientific need to know, leads me to reach out and touch a finger to his back. He gives two quick, thrusting kicks of his hind legs and then pulls himself back exactly into his former position. This irrevocable evolutionary commitment to camouflage is like that of wood turtles I find on land, who will not alter the freeze-frame pose they take immediately upon detecting me (which is nearly always before I see them), even when they have stopped in midstep, unless I actually touch them. But the turtle has a court of last resort, one adaptation left when going unseen has failed: his shell. The treefrog would seem to be completely defenseless once detected by a predator. I do not know whether this species has a final chemical ploy, a skin secretion like that of a toad or red eft, that would deter a predator from taking it in its mouth. And I have even seen toads failed by their toxicity.

I cannot imagine finding a more occult treefrog, though there must be some I have been unable to descry in this quest. And I wonder how many turtles I have overlooked in my search for frogs. Any one thing intimately observed inevitably means many things left unseen. I shift back to a turtle focus and begin to read water and sedge and grass instead of emergent shrubs and saplings. I am elated at the discoveries I have made, at adding something of such significance for me to the bank of search-images I have been building since that long-ago boyhood day when I saw my first turtle in the wild. It is this deep fund of search-images, based on years of the most dedicated looking—though there is an intuitive aspect as well—that guides me as I continue to follow that trail through marsh and swamp, along river and stream.

⸙

INTERVAL

WITH RED DEER

10 JUNE, 6:35 A.M. She is suddenly standing before me, the way it is sometimes with deer. As I look up from a long spell of reading the spare earth for signs of turtles nesting, the red doe, which my peripheral vision never picked up, is poised directly in front of me, out in the open. How does it happen that such an unconscious approach to this most wary and fleet-footed of animals is sometimes—rarely, but sometimes—possible? I have on some occasions had a deer approach me as I stood still. Did my manner of movement here, my blind-to-all-else absorption in inspecting the

ground somehow disguise me as a human, a potential menace? Does my intense involvement with my immediate surroundings allow me to pass as a part of the broader scene? During the best moments, I do enter into the day and become an aspect of all its workings.

She is posed like a postcard Rocky Mountain sheep atop a boulder near the crest of the long-abandoned sandpit. Set against a backdrop lush with the greens of a rain-rich spring, even along the impoverished borders of the sandpit, she is an almost burning red-sienna and yet is nearly lost against the dense-leaved tapestry of sweet fern and gray birch on the steep ascent just behind her. It is remarkable how the red of the whitetail deer in spring and summer can disappear so quickly, so completely, into the green of those seasons.

I hold still. She looks directly at me. There is something about this being regarded by a deer . . . I wear my camouflage shirt and earth-green warm-season waders, but she can hardly have failed to see me. (There is that face, those hands I always wish were not so conspicuous and often try to hide.) Utterly motionless, she holds her pose for a full two minutes. Without taking her eyes from me she begins to chew the bunch of leaves she holds in her mouth. There is no movement other than the working of her jaws as she finishes off her generous mouthful. I cannot make out what she is eating. It is not the green of the aromatic sweet fern that skirts the great stone she stands upon—that would be a morning tonic. Then, within that consummate stillness, her ears turn slightly, now both at once, now each separately, scanning, interpreting sounds in a morning moment that to my ears is pure silence. Another three minutes pass (moments of stillness in a presence such as this are a different kind of time, extended time), with no more movement than the slow shiftings of her ears, occasional blinks of her large, dark, moist eyes, and the subtle rhythmic movement of her belly as she breathes.

We are so close to each other that I can see these subdued signs of life quite clearly. Her eyes, ears, and nostrils are filled with the morning . . . her mouth has the taste of it. Her eyes take in the early light of the day, everything in the landscape before her with a clarity I could never possess, a perception I cannot guess at. Her ears pick up whispers of sound I cannot hear, her nostrils detect scents I will never know. She reads the morning I have been trying to read. To have those senses—would I trade my thinking, dreaming, imagining mind for them for one full day, from sunrise through the day and night until the following sunrise? If I were able to make such a trade, would I ever want to come back, reverse the exchange and return to human sensibilities?

At length she turns and walks upslope, unhurried, graceful, silent, stands statuelike again at the crest, turns one more time and disappears, a red deer vanishing with absolute silence into the green.

NIGHT, DISTANT
LIGHTNING

12 JUNE. I move from the faint light that lingers in the great watery depression of the marsh to the lesser light of the spare, sandy, bluestem-tufted field at the edge of the wood, where turtles come to nest. By degrees the twilight fades. The reflecting marsh enhances the final light more than the pale field does; already the woods are cloaked in darkness. A massive silhouette darker than the night stretches across the northern horizon. Set against the sky it looks more like a mountain range than a mountain of clouds imperceptibly moving through. Above it expands a dome of open sky in which stars appear.

As I turn on my flashlight and begin to search the ground, faint flickers of light from the sky catch my eye, only to vanish before I can focus on them. Except for the moon and stars, one cannot look the night directly in the eye, for what is looked at straight on disappears and can be seen again only by a slight glancing away, a looking back just off to one side. But these capricious flashes—which, like the most ephemeral shooting stars, never seem to streak exactly where one is looking—are light; I should be able to catch sight of one. I begin to wonder if they might be the product of something in my own eyes.

But then I turn to see clearly a sudden, stronger flash within the distant cloudbank. Hardly has it gone out than a truly explosive light bursts within and illuminates a cloud-tower that ascends as the bright glow within it pulses. It burns out in complete silence, and I cannot make out the shape of the cloud. I turn off my light and watch a succession of strikes light up the upward-billowing thunderhead that encases them, exploding lights that surge successively brighter and then die away. The night's profound silence is magnified by the stunning display of this lightning storm within a cloud-mountain several miles away, celestial fireworks of a stunning magnitude.

Somewhere, I wonder just how far away, the earth is not so still. It seems strange—no hint of thunder, driving rain, or roaring wind reaches me, only the pulsing flashes of a

fury that rages within its own domain, moving through the
vast serenity of an early June night. With every burst of its
internal fires, the outer shape of this tower of exploding
lights is clearly delineated in the encompassing blackness
of earth and sky. I watch as this storm within clouds slips
slowly eastward, beyond the clear night sky and the brilliant array of stars that arch over my own place in the landscape. Have I ever known such stillness and silence as that
about me now?

I resume my search for nesting turtles. Later I see many
more distant flickerings off to the south. I keep an eye on
the starlit space between these clouds and watch for any
flashings approaching from the west. These cloud-worlds,
so beyond reach, seem to represent a realm of their own.
Yet they spring from the earth I walk, the water I wade;
they are bound to the world through which I drift in my
own earthbound way.

MEDICINE-SMELLING
EARTH

13 JUNE, 5:30 P.M. Almost upon my arrival to begin another evening search for nesting wood turtles, I come upon
one on a nearly perpendicular slope. She has an ambitious
dig in progress. I had scanned all areas diligently with binoculars before walking out into the open, but she was con-
cealed by a slight ridge. Something in the way these turtles
orient themselves as they travel, in the way they hold still,
then move again, move without moving, it seems, enables
them to appear by surprise at my very feet, not just in heavy
riparian cover or densely brambled field-edge habitat but

in open terrain, even sandpits and riverine sand and cobble bars. Wood turtles are cliff dwellers at nesting time. If she nests here, though, it will be in the most precipitous nest site I have ever observed. Now, as I walk along lower ground, I see where she made an earlier ascent and moved along a steep incline just below the overhanging turf at its crest.

Rain appears imminent; this often inspires wood turtles to move out to nest, sometimes even at midday. They seem

Wood turtle nesting in the rain.

to know when rain is due within the next twenty-four hours, even when there is no sign of it that I can read. If her impressive trail, so clearly etched in sand, is not washed away, I should return tomorrow to photograph it.

Half an hour later, as I circle back along the edge of the hayfield, I see that the turtle I found digging earlier has come up over the crest of the slope. I regret I've come too close to her once again. She has already seen me, and it is too late to do anything but walk on by. Evidently she is continuing her search for a nest site. As I move away and descend the slope, I find several trial digs and an abandoned chamber, the work of the same agile turtle, I suspect.

Running, that is, hurrying in my turtlelike imitation of running, up the last fifty yards of the gentle incline of the old logging road, I just beat a heavy downpour to my car. My history at turtle-nesting time is marked by dodging thunderstorms, twice being overtaken by swift and violent ones, and being pinned to the earth by them. I had heard this one coming for a few minutes, that roar like a sudden wind, an almost trainlike sound in the trees, though all around me was breathlessly still. Though not far off, the sound came from the south, and I thought the east–west drift of the rain would have it pass by me. But then, seeing the near landscape go silver with heavy rain, I made my move just in time. I should know by now not to shave these margins so closely. Rain pounds my car as lightning cracks and thunder roars. I would want more shelter than a poncho and my own skin in this tempest; it's lucky that I was far closer to this refuge than I usually am in my wanderings.

The storm furies off to the west, and the rain abates; I walk in a steady drizzle as it quiets away. The hard-packed dirt road is a shallow, swift-running stream. Footprints and turtle trails, all signs of nesting, have been washed away. I had been wanting a clean slate to read, as my footprints from previous days' wanderings, along with the turtles' trails and trial diggings for nest sites, the tracks of deer, and excavations by egg-seeking predators have made it difficult to distinguish signs of fresh nesting activity. It is warm and still, silent except for distant rumbles of thunder now and again.

Mercifully, the mosquitoes have not yet come out into the open air, though it is cloud-darkened and steamily humid. Rain-scented air, medicine-smelling earth, silence now interspersed with faint bird calls from across the hayfield, stillness broken at moments by slight stirrings of wind, so imperceptible that the slender grasses seem to move on their own. How loud the droning of a bumblebee some distance off among the blackberry flowers. Thunder rolls again. It is to the north and east, moving away; for a time I can walk without rain.

WITH THE GRAY FOX

EDGING MY WAY along the eastern margins of a peatland that is about a mile and a half long and variously a fifth to a quarter of a mile wide, I try to pass unseen by those traveling the busy roadway that runs along the entire length of the fen. Painfully close, the pavement is generally less than fifteen yards from the wetland border. I can bring myself to be here only by virtue of the extremely dense cover that occupies most of this narrow margin, a barrier of buttonbush, sweet pepperbush, sapling and occasionally mature red maple trees, a near-impenetrable woody structure made all the more formidable by being bound up in stout-thorned common greenbrier.

This cover shields me from a world very different from the peatland, which, with deep reluctance and many misgivings, I have agreed to investigate. I am loath to do suburban turtle work, but some individuals and the local conservation commission have asked me to document the presence and seasonal movements of spotted and Blanding's turtles. Road-killed spotted turtles have been found here—I saw the shell of a three-year-old—and the Blanding's are strongly suspected to inhabit the peatland and its surroundings. These two species are declining primarily because of habitat loss and are considered of special concern throughout their ranges. Proof of their presence might provide a bit of leverage to gain concessions from a suite of developers poised to press upon the entire western side of this remarkable ecosystem, some backing off that might spare a measure of the habitat margins. I have conducted such field investigations before and have seen my evaluations and recommendations all but invariably come to naught in terms of any truly meaningful protection. Pointing this out and elucidating scenarios from my personal history, in which "information/documentation" and "education" have time and again proven not to be the answer, I sought to avoid this engagement. (There will come a time when I can no longer become involved in such campaigns at all.) But once again a conscientious group has sought my perspective, and I have agreed, for the nature of this peatland intrigues me. There is also the fact that paid turtle work is uncommon and sometimes hard to turn down.

The greater portion of this boglike wetland is untraversable. I thrust my five-foot wading stick down into a pool surrounded by sphagnum laced with sweet gale, a rafting that shakily supports me, without touching anything solid. My course is dictated by a circuitous route in which I can find enough footing to sink no more than waist-deep and by my efforts to keep a concealing screen between me and the road. The growth in this acidic fen, dominated by leatherleaf and sweet gale, is generally no more than waist-high. By wading mucky channels that are not bottomless, I can shorten myself and thereby attempt to avoid detection by passers-by as well as by the turtles I hope to see before they see me. It is decidedly "advantage turtle" here.

My only other ally in achieving stealth is my customary trait of moving slowly and holding still for periods of time. Houses have been built on the upland peninsulas thrusting from the roadway into the wetland, and I feel all the more exposed to human eyes as I explore a backwater cove between two of them.

As I stalk turtles who may or may not be here—so much of the time I search for the invisible, and for much of that time the object of my search may not even be present—a shadowy, silver gray movement catches my eye. I make out a small fox in a welter of shrubs and greenbrier who is intent upon a grackle which, in quest of his own food, is tossing leaves about in a tiny clearing. With extreme, rather catlike stealth, the gray fox inches forward, employing the upland-border screen, as I do, to pass unseen, but he steals through it with consummate grace and complete silence. The coloring of his pelt is far more concealing than the camouflage shirt I wear. He is one with sunlight and shadow, the grays of the shrubs, fawn and sienna of fallen leaves, a beautiful ghost of a predatory mammal who is alternately there and not there even when moving. I am in a zone of open water and low-growing leatherleaf; the shoreline vegetation must block me from his vision. I freeze the moment I make him out, and he goes statue-still at the same moment. Does he sense me? Or is he reckoning his approach to the preoccupied but doubtless alert grackle? The jet black bird gleams iridescent purple and gunmetal as he goes about his foraging on the floor of the thicket.

The fox makes an additional increment of advance. With a burst of his wings the grackle takes flight and vanishes at once. A large bird for such confining quarters, he has his own ways of navigating branch mazes and weavings of thorny vines. The fox, who has been in something of a crouch, stands erect, on tiptoes even, his large ears also erect, and stares at the place from which his prey has disappeared. He opens his jaws wide and runs his tongue over his shiny black lips, as though tasting the bird he was unable to get hold of. Then he moves off a bit and settles himself in a small hollow at the base of a wild apple tree that has somehow found a footing in this narrow jungle. He curls up and wraps his tail around himself.

My back has become painful, though I have straightened it a bit at times and shifted my weight from one foot to the other when it seemed the fox wouldn't notice. There are only tiny windows in the mazes between us. He looks directly at me for a moment . . . his face appears and disappears with slight turnings of his head. For seconds at a time, we seem to look right at each other. I look straight into his almost dreamlike eyes, see clearly his fine features, beautiful coloring, narrow muzzle, and sharp, black-tipped nose. Once again I feel that my own pale face must be conspicuous, out of place even. But he does not appear to make it out.

Across the road the woods are gone, replaced in the turning of a single year by fifty half-million-dollar houses, acres and acres of lawn set with forlorn trees left standing in isolation here and there, driveways, and wide avenues named for what once may have been there: Trillium Way, Ferncrest Drive, Birch Lane. Perhaps somewhere in the interior of the development a road has been named for the fox. No contribution to any architectural legacy, the houses seem embarrassed, standing in a twilight zone of suburban landscape, awkwardly, blankly, staring at each other across empty space. It will go worse for the fox when this landscape conversion is mirrored in triplicate on the other side of the peatland. He will be compelled to adapt even further, dodging automobiles as he hunts the narrowest wetland edges and backyards, mostly by night.

The fox and I are between two houses and not far in from the road. I look up over a mound of highbush blueberry off to one side to see a woman turning the pages of a book as she sits on her deck, which overlooks the wetland. I am extremely ill at ease. The gray fox yawns as he lounges in his open-eyed siesta. It does not appear that the woman will finish her book anytime soon. Not wishing to cause suburban terror, I slink in the direction of the second house, where no one seems to be about. It is so much easier for the fox to run this gauntlet, to slip the network of human eyes and move without being seen.

The difficult growth in this treacherous fen is too low to conceal all of my movements. I have been sighted. As I go on with my searching, I note the slow passings of a police car, and I understand better than ever why they are called cruisers. When I return to my car at the edge of the road I receive the company I was expecting. The black-and-white police car pulls up behind me and two uniformed officers get out. I am certain that my own uniform of black headband, camouflage T-shirt, and waders did nothing to allay the concerns of a crime-watch neighborhood. I am asked for my driver's license and social security number and then told to explain what I am doing. I state my mission and mention local contact people. After radio checks are made, I am thanked for my cooperation. There is one final question, which I had also anticipated: "What's with the basketball?"

As I left the wetland, I found a basketball that had escaped down Trillium Way and bounced far enough out onto the quaking sphagnum mat to prohibit its being retrieved and had decided I would take it home to give to some young friends.

"We thought maybe you had it in case you fell in."

VARIABLE DANCER

12 AUGUST. I make out a little pickerel just beneath the surface of the brook, his green-gold barring used to excellent effect in blending with the scant submerged and surface blades of bur-reed that trail from the downstream tail of a sandbar; he is a fish more gold than green, with a thin line of pale bronze drawn from snout to tail, as straight as a pickerel. Slender vertical bars (like the finest underwater reticulations of burnt bronze sunlight glimmering over the sandbar) are spaced along his sides. So many living things live on by keeping close to, disappearing into, something that looks so much like them, at times exactly like them: sunlight and shadow, water and earth, sand, stones, plants living and dead. Pattern is such an integral part of the pattern.

A pair of ebony jewelwings is nearby, poised on a broad-leaved overhang of fox grape and silky dogwood, she resting her white-tipped dark wings and he his jet black ones above their burnished-metal bodies . . . fish and damselflies, jewels set in a sunlit run of the brook at midday.

My progress along the stream arrested by the little fish that caught my eye, I set up watch here in the heavy cover of overhanging shrubs and vines. But I am not long taken up with fish and damselfly, for I see an orange flash in the water, the thrust of a wood turtle's leg. A small turtle struggles to hide in, or perhaps simply pass through, a weaving of silky dogwood stems directly beneath my watching place. I step down into the stream and pick him up. The pickerel darts away at my first movement, but the damselflies keep their places.

I hold the turtle up to the sunlight for inspection and note at once that half his tail is missing. But I have him in my hands a full minute before I see that his right front leg is gone; not the slightest stump remains. His left front leg is pale white where orange and black scales have been chewed away. But the leg and foot are intact, not a toenail missing. On the orange-scaled bases of his hind legs and right heel, scorings seem to have been made by tiny, needlelike teeth. There are no tooth marks on his shell. Whatever predator it was that took his leg—obviously not something as large as an otter—knew that gnawing on the shell of a turtle, even one this small, would be to no avail. Although they are quite fresh, the wounds, even at the amputated leg, are not bleeding. I suspect that he was attacked on land and has taken to the brook to hide and heal. He is in his seventh growing season. We have met before: he bears tiny notches in his marginal plates I have made to identify him as wood turtle number 105 in this populous colony, which I have been looking in on for twenty years. Somewhere in my notebooks are records of previous encounters, perhaps from the time the turtle was a hatchling. I return him to his cover in the stream. If both of us continue on here, I may come upon him as a three-legged adult thirteen or more years from now, may be able to find this record in my notes, and know to within a few days when he lost his leg.

My turtle discovery of the day is not a happy one. But I think again of how often something is revealed simply by my coming to these places. This is especially true in the complex of wetland, riparian, and upland habitats of which this brook is a vital component, a diverse and relatively isolated landscape with which I have a deep bond. Such a bonding can never be long enough or intimate enough, the way it is with any love.

I cross to the exposed crest of the small sandbar, scattering three newly transformed green frogs, all carrying the final traces of their tail stubs. The bar is crowned with rice cutgrass; two little clumps of a sedge are beginning to flower. The little pickerel who was poised here has not returned. My adventure with the wood turtle has driven him from his watery hunting ground for the time being.

I continue to search the water. But it is something in the air that next catches my eye, a drift of color that is there and then not, in the deep shade around me. It appears again. I strive to follow this seemingly disembodied flicker of violet that is both striking and invisible over the streamside shallows. Can color come to life? Here is a living thing I cannot even catch with my eyes. Then I do catch sight of, and manage to follow to where it comes to rest, a tiny damselfly, a variable dancer. And how variable this dancer is: a wisp of color, lavender dancing in shade along a wooded stream, a tiny shadow moving in the transparent colorlessness of the absence of sunlight over dark, wet sand.

Because a small fish and a pair of jewelwings caught my attention, I found a wood turtle, and because I stopped to look at a wood turtle I saw a variable dancer. For a time I have been united with all of them, by my sight, my being here, by whatever it is that brings me to such places time and time again. They are connected with one another and with everything else out here by the streaming of the brook and a coevolutionary history that is yet being written. And they are linked by a moment shared in time, a moment that I myself can share and so become connected with a world that could seem so far apart.

WALK TO
THE FLOODPLAIN

24 AUGUST, AFTERNOON. My one somewhat domestic link with the river comes by way of two seasonal streams that cut through woods on our property and pass along the northern and eastern borders of a level field behind our house. The field is predominantly wild, with bluestem grass, barren strawberry, bristly dewberry, goldenrod, and native shrubs, but we have set gardens in it here and there. The brooks join at the northeast corner, follow the wooded eastern edge of the field, then run down a steep, wooded de-

scent of half a mile or so to a confluence with the river. This watercourse, so near at hand, is one I seldom follow, in part because, within that half-mile run to the river, the conjoined streams have to pass through culverts, first at the base of a high berm erected to accommodate a state highway and then, not far below that, under the northbound lanes of an interstate that was run through the river's narrow floodplain thirty-five years ago.

Today, as I do every few years, I follow the seasonal stream's bisected cut to the floodplain. By late summer of most years, the brook has gone dry, yet the black silt that lines the level runs along the field is wet, the substrate a never-drying muck. A steep tumble of stones, moist with moss and humidity, drops from the southwest corner of the field's plateau. It is an icy staircase in winter, a rushing waterfall at thaw and after hurricanes or remnants of a tropical storm at summer's end. This silent tracery in the landscape can be brought back to rushing-water life by rainy spells at any season.

I gingerly descend the abrupt, slippery stairway of stones. A third of the way down to the floor of the great hollow into which it drops, I step onto a level rim about three feet wide that encircles the hollow. The steep berm of the state road cuts through the outlet end of this great bowl, which was shaped in the earth by ice and running water. The rim is evidence of the workings of the glacier, the original landscape designer and engineer of the topography through which I pass.

The contours of the hollow suggest how it came to be. At the breakup of the last ice sheet, during the era that configured the landscape of the glaciated Northeast—a landscape richly laced with waterways—a huge block of ice lodged here, one of the chunks left behind by the eroding glacier. For a time the torrents of meltwater that cut the stream channels here divided around the persistent ice, depositing deep alluvial sand and forming the rampart on which I stand. Over greater time the ice block itself was scoured away and disintegrated entirely, leaving this hollow in the earth, the negative space of its former self.

Today, in this silent space left so long ago, I can envision that block of ice with water racing around it, the erosion and deposition that created the hollow and its broader surroundings. Perhaps the ice let go all at once, crushing and shifting stones, or perhaps gradual melting and insistent erosion over time created the ravine that descends to the floodplain, itself shaped by the dynamics of the river's flood pulse. There is a reckoning of time on which a millennium is a minute. Ten thousand years ago can seem like yesterday in a place like this—a place of earth and water, time and the seasons.

The layers of white pine needles lining the descent are even slipperier than the wet stones. With the assistance of handholds on smaller trees, I make my way down the wall left by the ice block. I come to the floor of the depression, where over more recent time mucky organic sediments, the stuff of swamps, have been building up. If I were to block the entrance to the culvert and use the berm as a dam, I could turn the hollow into an impoundment almost twenty feet deep and fifty yards in diameter. Because of the workings of water over the year, trees cannot grow here. It is a realm of moss and fern and, in central spaces more open to the sky, marsh marigolds and marsh blue violets, which bloom before the leafing out of the deciduous trees that line the slope. This is another of those places, or spaces, in which I like to stand and be still for a time. It is no great precipice I have come down, but I am not fond of, nor well suited to, the ascents and descents required to get here. And then there is the roadway. But the world goes by up there . . . goes on by. It does not stop to look in, much less enter. Even the noise of the world passes overhead, or at least enough of it that in this hidden hollow on the edge of everything I try to avoid I can yet find the stillness and silence in a remnant of the natural landscape I am constantly searching for. This place is emblematic of what the black bear and moose, even the turtles and frogs, have been left with. But it is the human erosion of the landscape, a far different work from that of the glaciers, that drives all of them, great and small, into narrower and narrower corners of the world.

I think of how often I am in an arena of life, for every place in nature is a theater. What dramas have played out upon this little stage, what scenes of long duration or fleeting moments? Time is ever passing by, yet here it seems also to stay. Minutes, hours, can hold their breath in this stillness. Seasons hold in place even as they move through the year. How much water in how many forms has rushed or slowly drifted through here, lingered here? And the living tide as well, of plants and animals, all the kingdoms of life.

Water routes, from oceans to slips of seasonal water like this, have served over deep time as life's migration corridors. Despite the highways, even the largest animals of the day—bear, moose, white-tailed deer, coyote—continue to move along this cut. Their seasonal movements are not optional; they have no choice but to run every gauntlet, from backyard to superhighway, that unceasing human engineering and manipulation of the planet put in their paths. I know the larger mammals almost entirely by their footprints, for they maintain their ancient secrecy, hiding from man even in the unconscionably marginalized contemporary landscape. Night, even though illuminated by artificial light that can be seen from outer space, continues to be an ally in the clandestine shiftings of these animals. The same function is served by floodplains, other wetlands, and wilder streamsides, where any remaining cover tends to be the thickest.

I find evidence of the animals' passing through. One morning, in a small plot I had turned over in my back-field garden the previous evening, I found a record of those I rarely see, the tracks of a bear, moose, deer, and coyote. I doubt that they had formed a parade, traveling almost in each other's footsteps, but between dark and dawn all had walked over the same small space along their common way. Their tracks were all but superimposed upon each other; I could frame them in a single photograph. Smaller animals following the travel corridor of the ravine are killed on the state road, and they and the largest, bear and moose, are sometimes found as roadkill on the highway.

I climb up the virtually perpendicular wall of the berm, cross the first road, and go down into the steep, rocky ravine that will lead me (with a cautious crossing of the interstate) to the floodplain. As I pick my way among the stones, I see a fan of broad, blue-gray feathers. Startling pieces of a scattered puzzle quickly come together as I make out the remains of a freshly killed great blue heron. The remnants are almost indistinguishable among the muted tones of leaves fallen long ago and the blues and grays of shadow and stone: a shoulder and part of a wing here, a spray of wing feathers there, a leg, the long, curving neck, dismembered parts lying within a few feet of one another. I cannot imagine how this great-winged bird of the open sky, long-legged wader of broad expanses of open-ceilinged wetlands, came to a violent end in a dry streambed beneath a dense canopy of trees. There are no fish or frogs to hunt here; this is no place for a four-foot-tall heron to land. Or was he struck in high flight and brought to earth here? It is as though a piece of the sky has fallen. I can't think of any habitat suited to a heron in this vicinity . . . or was he heading for the river? It is strange how seldom one finds the larger animals dead, save for the endless carnage of road-kill. They are secret even in meeting death. From what I make of the remains, this was a heron in his prime. I often wonder how a heron, or a deer or bear, having survived the vulnerable first or second year, does come to an end. Unable to solve the puzzle I am looking at—feathers, bits of bone, dried blood—I regard it as a graphic testament to the great blue heron's final flight.

I find his head and bill. The skull, which is slightly chewed, more likely the work of a scavenger than of what brought him down, is little more than a knob at the base of a long blade, an ornament serving as the handle of a sword. The bill itself has a narrow split in the middle that runs its full length. A narrow line of brilliant yellow borders this crack, which suggests the force of whatever bite or strike brought this bird to ruin—or was it caused by a fall from the sky? Except for the skull of a large snapping turtle (it looks much like the head of a sea turtle), I am not a collector of skulls. But I pick up this once-living sword to give to a friend who studies and photographs birds, and walk on.

As I enter the floodplain, I follow deer trails through shoulder-high sensitive fern that seems, like so much that grows in such habitats, out of scale. Or I should say that the vegetation dwarfs me; I am the one out of scale here. I come upon several broad, matted—crushed, even—open areas around some of the towering, many-trunked stands of silver maple. These trampled clearings look far too large

Young-of-the-year water snake.

There are elements within elements in the floodplain... or I should say worlds within worlds. A bend in the river, cut off long ago as the restless water changed its meandering course, has become an oxbow. It now holds that aura of timelessness so characteristic of a marsh in late summer. It is so still, serene. How can there have been long months of ice and snow here, and the turbulent floods of thaw, when this oxbow was indistinguishable from the river? Ice & snow melt... the water settles out and the marsh reappears, so rich in life at this hour that summer could seem eternal. I stare into one small space: waterlilies; bullfrog; young-of-the-year watersnake, so strikingly banded; and a painted turtle, head-up among lily pads crossed by shadows of sedge and bur-reed. He does not so much as blink during the long while I regard him, in that unmoving turtle trance I have tried to outwait at times, all but never with success. Does time stand still with them? They appear transfixed by the sun, possessed of a patience well beyond the greatest I can summon.

to be places where deer, or even moose, have bedded down. They seem unquiet in the great green silence here. Are they arenas in which some vital contest took place? At this season it would probably have been the contest of predator and prey rather than a jousting for mates; but there are no bits of fur or bone, no traces of blood. And yet the tale of some great struggle appears to have been written in the monu-

Painted turtle among lily pads.

mental space and silence of this floodplain. For me it would take some effort and a club, at least, to make such an impression in the junglelike vegetation here, even though none of it is woody, except for the silver maples.

I stand so often where much has taken place and will yet take place, events I have little knowledge of. And what is going on even at the moment I stand here, which I have no way of knowing? From the high tree canopy to the dank, alluvial earth, the growth is rank and interwoven; all plants become one plant in the high-summer floodplain. There is space at the edge of the river. I look up at blue vervain, with its cobalt spires set against the milky blue of the August sky. A ruby-throated hummingbird alternately darts and holds still in the humid air, piercing the crimson throats of the cardinal flowers, vibrantly red against the endless green.

The river cuts deeply, darkly, around a right-angle turn here. Submersed plants I cannot identify undulate slowly, rhythmically, in great masses of long strands draped in algae. There are small fish here, dark shapes for a moment, then no more than tails disappearing, forms dissolving in greater darkness. The shallow water of summer (it is almost impossible to remember the spring floods), so slow moving as to be virtually still along this amber-gold, nearly level

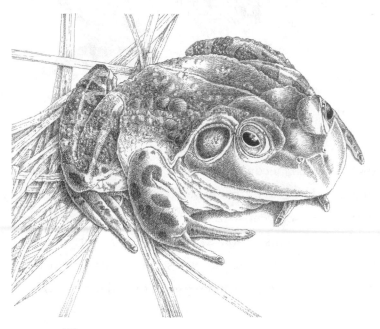

Bullfrog.

Water lily.

lowland reach, becomes restless at the deep-bend meander. Quickened by gravity and the extreme turn of its bed, much of the river's current swirls out of sight beneath an undercut bank. It seems to hold secrets here, some private work it is up to, this river that knows so much of the workings of earth and water, life and seasons, over deep time.

A DRINK ALONG
THE WAY

BLAZING SUN on sand, midday August heat. I head for the deep shade of a tall stand of white pines that tower on the crest of a ridge dropping to the wood-turtle stream. In this direction the pines are flanked by low wetland shrub thickets. Opposite, off to the west, extends the broad, level, open plain of an abandoned sandpit, where the earth has been stripped to a bare mineral layer bordered by slopes steep enough to be walls.

It is ninety degrees, welcome heat that in a time of year free of plaguing mosquitoes and black flies allows me to wear a single thin camouflage T-shirt. For so much of the turtle season, I am obliged to wear layers against the chill and/or biting insects. I come to this shade at noon in the time of the wood turtles' hatching. Over the years I have found them here often enough, by turtle-seeking standards, to believe that the little ones emerging from nests on the sand flat or slopes orient themselves toward the dark shape of the pines and their great communal shadow. So I look here first, before I take up my crisscrossing of the heated open terrain.

In this place the word *arena* works both literally and figuratively; *arena* in Latin means sand or sandy place; in Spanish, the word is used for sand, but also for bullring or stadium, a place for a spectacle. In this theater of sand the rituals and dramas of wood-turtle nesting (from late May into June) and hatching (from mid-August into September) are played out.

And here today I have another of those encounters that draw me to the arenas of the turtles. After first searching the pine-shaded ground, I cross the sharp demarcation of the shadows' outer extent and step into the blinding sun where, the moment my eyes adjust, I see a hatchling wood turtle, barely over an inch long. He is not many shell lengths short of reaching the shadow of the pines. What long, hot, dusty way has he traveled? I once found a hatchling close to where this one has settled, having seen me before I saw him, on the sand. That earlier hatchling, though perfect in every regard, was dead. Even his gesture was full of life, but he had died in midstep, literally stopped dead in his tracks, on a nest-to-water journey that could go no farther. I could only conclude that he had succumbed to overheating in his effort to reach the shade.

I pick up today's tiny traveler and move back under the pines. This one does not appear to be under stress, but I feel I should take him out of the sun to document him. And I would be blinded by the glare reflected from my notebook pages were I to record him out in the open. I take my balances and calipers out of my vest to weigh and measure him. Ordinarily I simply set a turtle back in place after I make my notations, as I always try to stay in the role of observer. But it occurs to me to offer this turtle some water.

The hatchling has been in a chamber in the sand for more than seventy days, encased in a shell until his recent pipping from the egg and subsequent digging out of the nest. There has been no rain in more than two weeks. His only drinking—if it can be called that—has come from hydration provided by the contents of his mineral-coated eggshell and its absorption of moisture from the sand, replenished at intervals by rain during the protracted incubation period. I take my water bottle out of my backpack and use the plastic cover of the casing that holds my calipers as a shallow dish. I set the turtle down and place the egg-tooth-tipped point of his upper jaw in contact with the water. The instant this seemingly magic touch is made, the hatchling extends his neck full length, immerses his head, closes his eyes, and begins to drink. This turtle has never seen, never tasted, water in this form. But he knows it at once, just as his mother knew at once the sandy terrain she needed when she set out on her first nesting expedition when she was about twenty years old.

The hatchling's throat shows the slow, steady pumping of his drinking. He is oblivious to everything but water, that medium essential for life—the enormous being that picked him up and carried him off, the suite of instincts and senses that has been guiding his survival, directing that first monumental experience with his natal planet, his nest-to-water journey, even any concept he might have of danger. Nothing but this first full drink of water matters now. Minutes go by. His head is still immersed, his eyes closed, neck fully extended, throat rhythmically pumping. I can feel this turtle's elemental thirst. I come to a deeper understanding of need in the natural world and wonder what limits this outwardly untroubled wanderer had been taken to.

Having decided to time this long, deep draft, I catch up on my notes while keeping an eye on him. Five minutes go by . . . ten . . . he does not open his eyes, does not come up for air. After twenty-one unchanging minutes of drinking, the hatchling lifts his head from the water and opens his eyes.

DANCING TREE

I WALK LONG, late September shadows again today, and again today light breezes are at play in them. I feel the heated sun in open-field places and in sun-slants among the shadows. I see a young girl dancing. It is the wind in a sapling big-toothed aspen, turning golden leaves over to shimmer with sun reflected from their pale undersides. She dances a moment in an open space, with little bluestem grass bronzing all around and gray goldenrod fading to seed on the sand flats where hatchling wood turtles have departed from their nests. She stands still, a sapling again, just for a moment, and then is dancing leaves once more, a young girl dancing on the restless wind, so supple, swaying and bowing in her circumscribed place in this clear field with crickets singing. As I read these signs of another season (I am old enough now that they seem an ancient personal history), the sun and the sand and the wind in the leaves and the dancing girl who cannot stay, a silent voice within me asks, as it has every autumn since I was a small boy, "Where does the season go?" And then asks the season, "May I go with you?"

HAWK-STRIKE

IT IS SO STILL that a red maple leaf touches down on the brook, alights on the slightest curl of one edge, and balances so. When a slight breath of air does stir, the leaf sets off, a small red sail on black water. It glides among bright shapes of sky scattered among the dark shadows that cover most of the surface in the late afternoon. The water is impenetrable to sight save where slants of sunlight find their way into shallows and impart an amber glow. One of these slants strikes the maple leaf, and for a moment it is a flame upon the water. I stand beneath a bower of wild grape, most of whose broad leaves have been eaten to lace, each one a delicate filigree of veins, a skeletal structure describing a leaf that no longer exists.

Suddenly the all-encompassing calm is broken by a bolt from above. A large hawk, with wings held close against his body and tail compressed, arrows through scant space from somewhere over my right shoulder, nearly grazing me as he streaks low across the brook on a deadly slant through a screen of shrubs to tangles at the base of a large red maple. There is the startling sound of air impacted by the braking of his wings, followed by a return to silence. For almost a full minute I hear nothing, see nothing. Then there is a rush of wing beats, and I glimpse a dusky shape vanishing in the undergrowth. The hawk—I'm quite certain it was a broadwing—has flown off at a level lower than my shoulders. I am struck by how skillfully this large raptor, a far more familiar sight wheeling, wide-winged, high in a great expanse of sky, maneuvers himself through these dense riparian thickets. He must, of course, come down to earth for the consummation of his hunt. Not long after the hawk's disappearance, a cadence sets up along both sides of the brook, up- and downstream: the rhythmic chuckings of chipmunks. As though beating low tribal drums, they signal one another.

As I heard no cry or sound of struggle, I presumed that the hawk had missed his target. Now I see a most agitated chipmunk zigzagging about on the rough-barked trunk of the red maple, several feet up from where the hawk struck. He chatters wildly. I could think he has a rather exciting tale to tell.

BROOK TROUT,
WOOD TURTLE

6 OCTOBER. I am a long time standing in the brook, at its edge, along a banking of royal ferns, my feet deep in a drift of leaves in a deadwater. I begin to wonder how many days are left in the year when I can enter the stream. Low in the water, close to the tops of my waders, I scan shallows and depths. As though they existed apart from me, my eyes descend to move in and out of shaded and sunlit pockets, root tangles, submerged lodgings of branches and drifts of sunken leaves. As always, my searching has a focus, a target. But as with my peripheral vision, peripheral thought as-

sumes a guiding role. Beyond the specific objective, nearly always a turtle or some aspect of turtle, there is a broader searching, whose specific object is something I have never been able to perceive, never had any need to know.

A brook trout appears. I didn't think my entry into the brook and even my motionless surveillance had been stealthy enough that I would suddenly find myself standing beside one of these elusive fish, so quick to vanish at the slightest movement. He was not there, or at least I did not see him, when I first looked in from my foothold atop the bank where, high above the water, my eyes could penetrate the stream more easily. Dark fish-shape, subtle motion, white fin margins, his shadow on the gravelly bottom . . . I don't know which I saw first or if all took shape at once. But all of a sudden I am looking at a trout who is almost exactly the color and tone of the sand-and-gravel bottom in the deeper, scoured, midstream channel. A little more than one stride away from my feet, he holds his place in the flow with a barely discernible undulation of his body and steadying of fins. From directly above, as he would be seen from a kingfisher's perch, he is no more than amber-olive movement in an amber-olive streaming. Trout suspended in, surrounded by, water ever flowing by, as I am suspended in, surrounded by, time ever moving on.

I turn my head to look at a small green frog who appears and disappears among floating and sunken leaves at the edge of the brook. When I look back, the trout is gone. A green darner, perhaps the year's last dragonfly, rattles over the swirling surface on wings beginning to tatter.

I pull myself up out of the water onto the bank, move upstream a bit, then step back down into the water just above the holdfast of a great royal fern mound. I set my right foot on the cobbled streambed and my left against the firm banking. Thus anchored, and steadied by one hand on my wading staff, I bend low to the surface and once again let my sight adjust and descend, to unravel the forms in the brook.

Almost immediately a pattern appears directly below me: fine ochery striations radiating somewhat symmetrically over the umber plates of a wood turtle's shell. This time it is not a defining bit of outline but the markings on the shallow central dome of a carapace, whose margins I cannot see, that reveal the turtle to me. Through a long coevolutionary history, this shell with its shadowy ground cast and unique markings has been designed by its surroundings to be part of, indistinguishable from, them. It is another of those living patterns that has been shaped by its chances of letting its bearer go unseen. I read just enough order to differentiate the pattern from the randomness in which it is set. The turtle's camouflage, deceptively simple, has been orchestrated to fit a far more complicated suite of surroundings and circumstances than those of the trout, for the camouflage must function wet or dry, in terrestrial and aquatic environments.

The brook trout has been designed by broken surface water, striations of sunlight in clear and tannic streams, and the gold and glitter of sand and gravel; the wood turtle, by all of these as well as by alder leaves and pine needles, wet or dry; shadows and flecks of sunlight in water or on land; dark, moist riparian earth; tangles of grass, goldenrod, and brambles; and screens of flood-drifted branches. With unfathomable complexity over time too deep to truly comprehend, species have been and are continuing to be shaped by each other and their environments and by the terms of existence brought to bear by the nonliving forces that govern their contemporary Earth. The continuity of this shaping and reshaping extends beyond the extinction of forms, body plans, and ways of being, as though all of life were one single determined mind, and each species that comes and goes were a different idea, directed toward persistence in a realm of constant change.

I reach into the brook, soaking the sleeve I cannot roll up far enough and immersing the lower right half of my vest. My face nearly in the water, I can see nothing. Shoulder-deep, I feel for the turtle with my numbing hand. Even in this cold water my fingers know the differences between roots and stones and turtle shells. I find the edge of the carapace and pull the turtle to the surface. His sculpted, stream-wet shell is, though earth-toned and subtle overall, rich with color: mahogany and lighter browns flecked with pale gold. The washes of brilliant red-orange on his neck and legs rival the spectral colors on the fins and sides of the brook trout. His wet black head glistens, and the gold ring of his wild eye gleams as it regards me. I quickly note the marks that identify this long-familiar, lord-of-the-waterway male and let him slip back into the stream. As he vanishes in patterns of swirling water and streambed colors, I wonder at those gold-ringed eyes of turtle and trout. What interpretations have they made of the world they share but have inhabited so differently since glaciers traced rivers and streams in a vast planet and filled them with the silver of ever-flowing water?

WADING ALDER BROOK

Water gives life to ten thousand things and does
    not strive.
It flows in places men reject and so is like the Tao.

—*Lao T̄ʒu*

WADING ALDER BROOK, I search a steep, west-facing
bank, just upstream from Willow Dam. The high, nearly
perpendicular slope rises twenty feet or so above the brook.
At its downstream base beavers built this dam but abandoned it long ago. A tenacious line of black willows, alder,
and silky dogwood colonized it, winding a massive network
into the mud-plastered woody structure, reinforcing and
eventually replacing the dam with a turfy embankment that
is breached by spring's unruly spates, whose silver cascades

bring life to a cutoff stream section. But in low-water autumn this natural levee deflects a steady slide of water through alder lowlands.

In scanning the mesmerizing play of light and shadow upon the brook and all along its banks, I feel as though I have a glimpse into the soul of the season. Set against the bank's slope, my own silhouette is alive with wavering lights, golden shimmerings in a slow-moving black shadow-shape. These rippling threads are sunlight tossed from a wind-ruffled quiet backwater just off the channel's more enlivened run, where water striders serenely glide. I see that the flickering reflections can come to light only in shadow. On the radiant slope of the sun-struck stream bank, they are invisible, lights dissolved in lights. Strewn with fallen leaves bleached of their autumn brilliance, the high banking has become a glowing ocher wall, a tabula rasa for watery writing.

Within every shadow, from that of the slenderest wisp of dried sedge to those of the infinitely branched debris of former floods and broader stems of standing alder and the one I cast myself (the largest among these), there is a ceaseless wavering of amber-gold webbings of light cast by flowing and windblown water. I move, and the lights move with me, glimmering wherever my shadow goes. I cannot catch them in my hand, but I can shift them about by playing the shadow of my hand over the stream bank and place them

where I will. It is as though the brook's reflections pass through me, pass through fallen trees and tumbled ferns. Sunlight and shadows, wind and water: at this late afternoon hour in deepening autumn the world becomes translucent, immaterial.

OXBOW MEANDER

Often on impulse, I walk out by myself:
Magnificent scenes, I alone know;
Walk to the source of the stream
And sit down to watch clouds rise.
                    — *Wang Wei*

THE SUN IS so low at this hour that it is all but impossible to look to the west, and I trail a long shadow as I make my way to the oxbow meander. Wood turtles at times take the last low sun of the year along its west-facing bank before entering the stream for their long overwintering. As I descend to the brook I see that a large red maple in the floodplain swamp has gone down, a casualty of yesterday's windstorm. This enormous windthrow obliges the deer to take another route among the ferns. And so it obliges me, as I borrow their new trail, a replacement of the former well-worn path that led me quietly and fairly easily to a ford in the stream. The tree's great tipped-up roothold has left a crater that seems destined to become flooded next spring, forming a vernal pool that may well be appropriated by wood frogs and spotted salamanders for their breeding.

The last warm days of autumn draw me to this place at the fading light of late afternoon in the evening of the year as does the breaking forth of spring, with its dazzling new light in the morning of the year. As fall moves on toward winter and the leaves begin to thin, the low shafts of light that are allowed to touch the stream and its banks become a deeply evocative testimonial to the turning of the year. Everything they touch is graced by a near-miracle radiance in the immediate landscape. The water is low and completely still, as it generally is at this time of year. The brook rests. The wild surges of March around the oxbow bend have been forgotten. Or remembered only, I see, in the swirls of grass and sedge and drifts of flood wrack, interwoven strewings of branches, stems, leaves, and vines that perfectly trace the course and mark the height of the flood that swept through the shrub thickets of the higher bank. In this artful-seeming arrangement of the wreckage of spring spates, as if the brook had left them here for the purpose, the wood turtles do their final sun worshipping of the year.

And here I find a turtle who has been doing just that. A young one has evidently been settled here for a while; several red maple leaves, let loose in the still air to spiral down from the high canopy, have landed on his carapace and stayed there, obscuring him all the more. The shadow from the high bank across the stream has crept over him as well. But the air is warmer than the water, and it appears that he will linger on the bank before returning to the stream, which, though only thirty-seven degrees, will be warmer than the air when the temperature falls below freezing in the night.

I find no other turtles—significantly, no adults—in this place that for so many years has yielded me many of my final sightings of the year. This could well be a reflection of the toll taken by the otter predation of last winter. I have unprecedented and unwelcome tallies among my notes for this season: I have, by way of four shells I found after discovering that first lifeless wood turtle at thaw, documented five fatalities. I know the seasonal movement patterns of at least half a dozen adults whom I would have expected to encounter this season but have not. And in addition to the known dead and those I have failed to come upon, who could well have succumbed to otter attacks, I have recorded upward of thirty turtles who have lost from half a leg to one or two entire legs.

And yet, in an alder- and meadowsweet-thicketed stream

reach a quarter of a mile downstream from the confluence of two brooks, the unusually populous wood-turtle center on which I have focused, I found four intact individuals, perfect to the tips of their tails. Because this site is in active farmland, I rarely go there. But I wanted to compare its wood-turtle status with that of the area of heavy impact. I cannot count this as a definitive survey, but I certainly have to consider that the predation may have been quite localized.

And perhaps episodic as well, if considered as an outbreak set in at least several decades of minimal predation. (Many of the adult turtles I have recorded were more than twenty years old when I began to observe this colony.) Space and time are clearly factors—I would say critical factors—in the coexistence of wood turtles and otters over millennia, an ongoing dynamic with so many variables and interactions and a complexity that may well be ultimately indecipherable.

Seeing, which I found so difficult upon my arrival, becomes nearly impossible as I follow a turn in the brook and face into the sun. Except in the shadows of the trees I am absolutely blinded. I see better after the sun drops below a ridge of white pines to the west. Then, as light begins to slip away altogether and I make my way from the brook, I gather pale kindling in the pine grove, smooth fallen branches from which all bark has sloughed. As I leave, as darkness deepens in the riparian landscape, a mood deepens in me of days growing shorter and the year ending. These transitions color me, as they have since my first boyhood wanderings, with a vague melancholy, even as they tinge the leaves of the streamside maples with an exuberant brilliance. I think back to a time long past when other brooks, now lost, ran wild, and I followed. Night comes on with its first small scattering of stars, and I forget what it was I was trying not to remember.

13 October – 1230h: after heavy rain yesterday afternoon-into-evening, clearing ... abundant sun, 10-20 mph winds, low 60°s classic conditions for late emergence by hatchling spotted turtles. On my way here I anticipated one lingering in a temporary rain pool, or even more than one in the flooded little low trough in Rose Pogonia Hollow. (It happens some years.) Find this one in shallows of North Fen, just off the ridge of deep wheel ruts made by the ATVs that roar through this wetland niche. Egg tooth has been shed and yolk sac scar is well-healed-over. Could have been on nest-to-water journey for some days, maybe in terrestrial hiding before the rain surge. Carapace scutes quite irregular, 13 marginals, left & right.
DMCARTO 9/

SLC 27.7mm
CW 26.2
PL 23.4
Wt: 4grams

173

FALLEN BUCK

18 OCTOBER. Walking up the autumn brook, I come upon a dead buck, a white-tailed deer lying on the mixed leaf-strewn and open mud of the bank. My eyes have been so intent on the water, and he is so well camouflaged—and so still in death—that as large as he is I nearly step on him before I see him. I have come close at times to living deer and have found several dead ones, in advanced decay or little more than bits of fur and bones; but I have never seen such a vision as this. Handsome in death, fallen somehow in his prime, he lies in a lifelike pose. His fur flows over his body with the grace of water flowing over stones in the nearby brook. His large ears—so large—which in life could

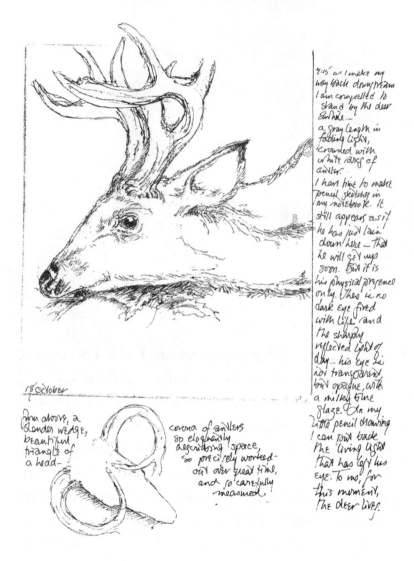

4:15 as I make my way back downstream I am compelled to stand by the deer awhile —

a gray length in fading light, crowned with white racks of antler.

I have time to make pencil sketches in my notebook. It still appears as if he has just lain down here — that he will get up soon. But it is his physical presence only. There is no dark eye fired with life, and the sharply reflected light of day... his eye is not transparent, but opaque, with a milky blue glaze. On my little pencil drawing I can put back the living light that has left his eye. To me, for this moment, the deer lives.

18 October

from above, a slender wedge, beautiful triangle of a head—

corona of antlers so eloquently describing space, so precisely worked-out over great time, and so carefully measured.

pick up the slightest whispers of distant sound, do not hear
the rushing of the water just beyond his muzzle. He would
make a perfect statue of a deer in gentle stride if I were to
right him. His hindquarters have been eaten at slightly . . .
there is some fresh blood and small scatterings of hair. I
take this as the work of scavengers and not what brought
him down. Even with these signs of inevitable dissolution
at his flanks he is so fresh and appears dignified in death.

As I admire his form and attempt to commit it to memory
—the sweep of gray, silvered, light fawn fur over his won-
derful rib cage—his sides seem about to heave with breath.
His large, wild shape and substance, in which a heart so
wildly beat not long ago, still speak of life.

I circle around him, looking from every angle, and each
view describes a perfection of form and function. I see how
the antlers he soon would have shed are securely set in his
head, their footings reminiscent of a tree's rootedness in
the earth. His antlers branch forth with a treelike twisting.
Taking the antlers in my hands—I never would have expected to have such a tangible hold on a deer, such a physical bond—I rock them and discover a surprising flexibility.
I raise his head and part of his muscular neck, lighter and
more supple than I would have thought. It seems his eyes
are about to blink, his nostrils twitch and snort. As I shift
his head about, I feel as though I could raise him entire, lift
him to his feet, and set him to run wild again . . . as though

I could even run wild with him, leap the brook with a single bound and run like a deer through the woods.

I gently lower his head and neck and settle them precisely back in the impression they have left in the semifrozen, leaf-lined brook-side turf, the shallow cradling depression where cheek and jaw rested (did the last of his animal warmth help shape it?) and walk on up the stream.

BROKEN GLASS

5 NOVEMBER. I see gleamings in the brook as I look into clear, chill water sliding over stones and cobble, gravel and sand, the streambed on which the wood turtles have settled as they begin to wait out another long winter. I find here one of the "books in running brooks" of which Shakespeare wrote, perhaps the one great book for me, one I never tire of trying to read. Now that successions of hard frost, cold rains, and wild late autumn winds have stripped the alders and silky dogwood of all their leaves, the stream is flooded with sunlight, except in runs through flats of white pine and along slopes of hemlock. Far more lit up than in deeply shaded summer, it is mostly a course through leafless miles,

its water filled with light even as the sun traces its low, edge-of-winter arc in the sky.

I could count the cobblestones that are magnified by this crystal streaming: dark stones and light and some that glint or give off a sheen when viewed from the right angle, mica, quartz, and feldspar. Something shines golden in the sand. Even if it were gold it would be but one more mineral among the many here. Raw or minted into coins, gold has no value in the economy of this wild-running stream. Only time can be spent here; it is the currency of the seasons and their workings, and all that one can ever spend here. The gleam of a gold nugget would signal no more value on the bottom of this stream than that of the soft, lustrous light given off by feldspar, the most common mineral on earth.

A spark of green arrests my eye. No emerald, a splinter from a shattered bottle catches a slant of sunlight. How has broken glass come to lie in a streambed this far from human habitations? The last earthly lights to mark that we were here on this planet, which we have illuminated to the point of fairly glowing in the dark of endless space, may be those cast by broken glass: brilliant sunsparks, bits of moon gleam, faint flickers of starlight, all reflections of the one original light.

BOUNDARY MARKER

AS I TURN toward the brook I am stunned by a sign. It is
not the kind of sign that I am ever on the lookout for, ever
trying to read on the earth, in the water, among the plants.
This is a human designation, a small rectangular boundary
marker nailed to a tree and bearing the initials of a land
trust. I knew this was coming, but I had no way to prepare
myself for it. And I knew it would go hard for me, but I am
surprised by the depth of my reaction, physical and mental,
to this symbol. It is almost enough to turn me back, send
me home. What will be regarded by nearly everyone as a
conservation victory, a cause for celebration, I can see only
as loss and sorrow. I had tried to steer this change in another direction, beyond conservation to preservation.

This landscape, an extensive mosaic of contiguous wetland, riparian, and upland elements, all embracing a lingering wildness and extraordinary biodiversity, possesses an ecological integrity that, in the face of the global loss and marginalization of habitats, becomes rarer by the hour. It seemed for a time that it could go differently here, that this place could be exempted even from the intrusion of "passive" recreation, which takes its own toll on wildness and brings pressures to bear on the functioning of a natural ecosystem. But I did see all the familiar signs pointing to this outcome. And now I see that this has become a marked place.

It is all but universally believed that if development rights are bought up and motorized vehicles excluded, if human presence is limited to foot traffic, dogs on leashes, mountain bikes, kayaks, and the like, a parcel of land is saved and its wildlife habitat protected. But in nearly every case, as will be true here, funding sources and the terms of easements mandate a level of access and recreational use that lays the foundation not for true habitat protection but for a playground for people, a human theme park.

A constant refrain of my advocacy for moving beyond stewardship and conservation to preservation is that I do support setting aside places where people can go, from relatively natural areas to city parks. One frequently hears that there are not enough places for people to go. But where do we not go? We are too many and we tread too heavily. (Perhaps the planet is to blame for being too small.) What tiny percentage of Earth is irrevocably dedicated to providing wildlife sanctuary, to preserving the biodiversity on which, as more people are gradually coming to realize, the health of the planet and, ultimately, of the human condition utterly depends? We cannot seem to allow room for ecosystems to play out their destinies free from human intervention. A room of its own is biodiversity's only requirement.

There is talk of a "nature-deficit disorder," the deleterious physical and emotional consequences of people's alienation from nature. The cure for this, as I have seen it addressed in various forums, tends to be simply getting out of the house and away from electronic pastimes. To this end, state parks are opened free of charge and present games such as "nature hunts" for children, and families are encouraged to provide their young with trampolines in winter and water pistols in summer. The distinction between "outside"—open spaces and multi-use conservation lands—and true preserves that provide sanctuary for ecologies becomes blurred and is ultimately lost. In this confusion the "natural" that remains in the landscape literally loses more and more ground and, with that, its meaning. It is nature that suffers from nature-deficit disorder.

A relationship, if not an outright union, with nature has

always been and always will be fundamental to the human spirit. But this connection, which has become so profoundly frayed in the modern world, must not be made at nature's expense. Earth cannot be expected to—and in fact simply cannot—bear the weight of a human population approaching seven billion and growing at the rate of some ninety million a year.

I walk past the metal marker and cross the brook. I had a premonition the last time I was out here when I saw a young wood turtle at the edge of a stream bank, in what was likely his final basking of the year, that I might be saying goodbye for more than a winter. I have seen this scenario play out before and have been compelled to move to more remote landscapes. But the world of the turtle species I have known runs out of farther landscapes. I see the clear possibility of my personal history with this wetlandscape—a long and intimate one—coming to an end.

As always, at the close of another season, I look to the thaw beyond the coming winter. I try again to reconcile myself to the fact that the fate of such places is up to the workings of deeper time, nature's own processes. The turtles, and all that they have come to represent for me, will have to endure. Spring will come again, and I will have to find a way to be there. My goodbye has always been until thaw.

As I cross the brook, I see spans of thin ice here and there on still edgewaters against the bank. This inevitable annual event somehow catches me by surprise every time. It is an undeniable signal of the year's passing. The waters of the fen at the north end of this wetland complex and the marsh beyond it are still open, but featherings of ice have begun to spread over the sphagnum shallows. It is so silent here today. Is it because there are no more insects to sing? The occasional stirrings of a bitingly chill wind are none the warmer for having passed over the glacial pond set in the heart of this wetland expanse. The wind makes no sound in its passing and seems to render the silence all the more striking. In every sense of the word the year is quieting.

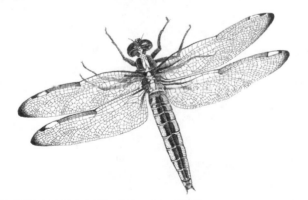

I wade into the great alder carr beyond the fen. There is a glazing of ice in the shallows, perfectly clear windows that I am sorry to shatter in my wading. For a time I shatter the silence as well, with sharp, crystalline sounds; then I wade to open water again and the day continues breathlessly still.

The low sun is a white disk in a smoked-glass sky: alto-stratus translucidus clouds. Ice, poised to march out over the open water in the night, rings the royal fern and alder mounds. I do not know if there will be one more mild spell; it is possible this will be the first and final closing over. The turtles may not move for half a year. If they stir at all, it will be beneath the ice. A couple of calls come from crows over distant pines, and then the profound silence returns.

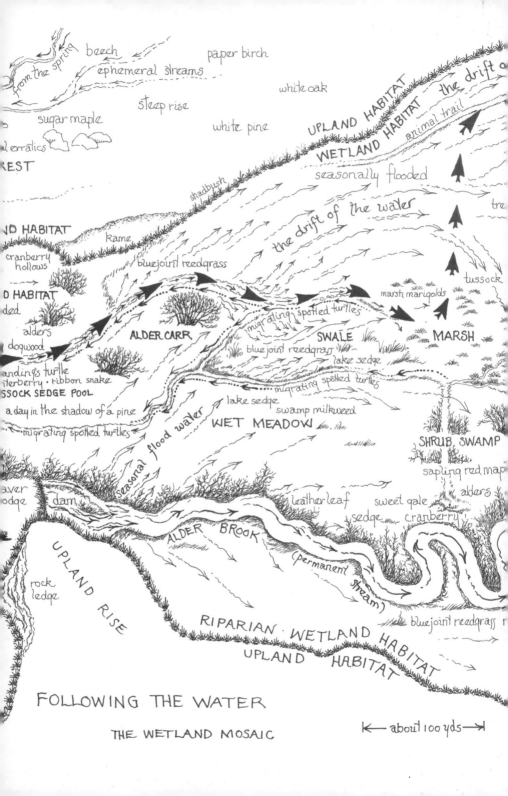

FOLLOWING THE WATER

THE WETLAND MOSAIC

|← about 100 yds →|